SYMBOLS   SIGNS   LETTERS

"Spoken words are the symbols
of the mind; written words are
the symbols of the spoken ones."

ARISTOTLE

SYMBOLS SIGNS LETTERS

MARTIN ANDERSCH

About handwriting, experimenting with alphabets, and the interpretation of texts

Experiences
Materials
Results

DESIGN PRESS

CREDITS

Paper: 150 g Praximatt
Type: Walbaum Book
Berthold AG, Munich/Berlin
Linotype Walbaum, Mergenthaler
Typesetting: Satzstudio Weishaupt, Meckenbeuren;
V & M Graphics, Inc., New York
Production: Appl, Wemding
Lithos: Photolitho AG, Gossau
Zurich, Switzerland
Cloth: Roughweave, Vereinigte
Göppinger-Bamberger Kailiko GmbH, Bamberg
Editor, German text: Astrid Hille
Photography: Fritz Peyer
Design: Martin Andersch
and Rudolf Göggerle
First published in German
SPUREN ZEICHEN BUCHSTABEN
© 1988 Ravensburger Buchverlag Otto Maier GmbH

English translation: Ingrid Li
© 1989 Design Press
First edition, first printing
Printed in Germany

Design Press offers posters for sale.
For information contact Mail-Order
Department. Design Press books are
available at special discounts for bulk
purchases for sales promotions, fund-
raisers, or premiums. For details
contact Special Sales Manager.
Questions regarding the content of
the book should be addressed to:
Design Press
Division of TAB BOOKS Inc.
10 East 21st Street
New York, NY 10010

Library of Congress Cataloging-in-Publication Data

Andersch, Martin, 1921–
    Symbols, signs, letters.
    Translation of: Spuren, Zeichen, Buchstaben.
    Bibliography: p.
    1. Calligraphy.   2. Penmanship.   3. Writing, Italic.
I. Title.
243.A55313   1989   745.6'1977   89-1532
ISBN 0-8306-5506-9

DEDICATION

To the School of Design at the University of Hamburg, in memory of the decade during which OTTO RUTHS *was dean.*

ACKNOWLEDGMENTS

Skriptorium Cormoran Hamburg

GERTRAUD BAUDY
RENATE FUHRMANN
ARMGART GROSS
MICHAEL KNIPPRATH
RÜDIGER MOHRDIEK
JENS RADEMACHER
ULRIKE STARON

GISELA ANDERSCH
FERNAND BAUDIN
REINHOLD BUSCH
DR. CHRISTOPH CARSTENSEN
PROF. DR. ROLF DALHEIMER
JOST HOCHULI
PAUL THEODOR HOFFMANN
BODO KAEMMLE
DR. PETER KAROW
WALTER KEMPOWSKI
VOLKER KÜSTER
GÜNTHER LANGE
GÜNTER GERHARD LANGE
GERRIT NOORDZIJ
FRITZ PEYER
ROSWITHA QUADFLIEG
RENATE RAECKE-HAUSWEDELL AND
DR. JÜRGEN RAECKE
PROF. OTTO RUTHS
PROF. DR. HELMUT SCHREIER
ECKEHART SCHUMACHER-GEBLER
URSULA AND GUNNAR SCHWEER
ERWIN STEEN
PROF. LORELOTTE WOLTER

IN MEMORIAM

ALFRED ANDERSCH
PROF. WILHELM MARTIN BUSCH
DR. HANNO HANSMANN
PROF. DR. ALFRED KANTOROWICZ
PROF. HUGO MEIER-THUR
REINHOLD MEYER
PROF. RICHARD VON SICHOWSKY

6

CONTENTS

This is a report on a more than twenty-year-long career dedicated to the teaching of European handwriting and to its ever-developing didactics. The field is applied art, as taught at a German university.

This is not a textbook. It is instead a picture book, a manual that makes visible the process of teaching and learning and the nature of the instruction process. The examples are exclusively the works of students, guests, and visitors of my evening seminars.

I offer this book to teachers in elementary and secondary schools as well as to professors at academies and universities. May it revitalize instruction, provide food for thought, give encouragement, and be a beacon in the desolation of contemporary education in handwriting.

The ministers of cultural affairs and education have neglected any intelligent and intensive teaching of handwriting in any applicable departments. Such neglect is foolish as well as dangerous, and should finally yield to the realization that our written heritage is an asset of extraordinary importance.

"An artist's mind works differently. He needs good common sense, but his heart, his feelings are purer and more prolific than his powers of logic. He relies more on his eye than on his calculations. His hand is more than just a tool, but a living thing animated and inventive. People of this kind think with their eyes and hands. Trained eyes and hands are a safeguard against stubbornness. They are variable and encourage variation. They age more slowly than the calculating intellect. They are devoted to what is close by, but they lead us to what is distant and unknown. They keep our desire to explore new things young, alive, and productive."

F. H. ERNST SCHNEIDLER

At the End of
the Twentieth Century

*The State
of Handwriting*

I

In the west we look back at two thousand years of development in the art of writing, not counting several thousand years during which the prototypes matured. We see a rich diversity of form that is constantly being redefined through creative variations, and it has lasted almost to the end of the twentieth century.

Two phenomena are responsible for the impending loss of aesthetic achievements in calligraphy and writing in general: handwriting as it is taught in school and the digital letters popularized by the electronic industry.

It is remarkable that both of these factors are manifestations of current trends in the development of writing.

The scripts that are taught in Europe, disgraceful examples of writing, prove that we are well on our way to analphabetism as we are renouncing the necessity of practice. Sadly, not much is left to be practiced. No help comes from the ministries for education and culture, where diffuse and uncoordinated guidelines for curricula originate.

A cultural value of the highest order should not be dealt with on a regional basis but internationally, to justify its importance.

Speaking/Writing/Reading, the trinity of our civilization, is threatened by neglect of writing. This process started a hundred years ago with Sütterlin. Students and teachers write equally badly, which is not surprising, since there is no formal instruction in handwriting after the elementary school years. Consider this shocking quote from the Brazilian teacher Paulo Freire: "As an old professor I can assure you that true analphabetism is rampant among students and professors alike in those institutions that call themselves universities."

Two things are accomplished by the invention of the alphabet, this most abstract and also most effective brainchild of man: It turns thoughts visible and preserves them at the same time. This noble discovery is treated indifferently in West German schools and its teaching descends to triviality at universities. Semantic sensitivity has to be employed to represent an aesthetic code, and practice has to be an integral element. Since practice requires time, the teacher has to demonstrate patience and affection towards the student. I quote from Helmut Schreier's essay "Das schöne Schreiben" ("Calligraphy"), (University of Tubingen, 1987). In the last paragraph of the chapter on practicing he writes: "Many a teacher who has involved himself with printing has had experiences with this kind of intensive practice. Arranging metal type and preparing it for printing requires a series of

"He who cannot interpret them right shall not cut runes."
EGLIS SAGA

precise movements and skills. Children will practice these skills over long periods of time, often with great devotion to the task, when they prepare a text of their own choice for printing. Would those children submit to the same repetitive exercises if they were not rewarded with a finished printed piece at the end of the process? Is this practice not the way to success? Is it not the essence of writing that it breaks through human isolation and unites us, defying time and space? We practice and we write and we pay with isolation, but we communicate with others; thus we overcome isolation. Should this experience not be accessible to one who practices writing? In the balance of aesthetic skill and communication lies the significance of writing! So much for the situation at our schools."

Suggestions and ideas to improve this unfortunate situation should be exchanged on an international, not an individual, level.

Dr. Peter Karow is the inventor of the Ikarus system, a computer program that stores letters and writing. He is also manager of an international business. In November, 1986, he gave me a copy of his newly published book, "Digitale Speicherung von Schriften" ("Digital Storage of Writing"), and he inscribed it with the following dedication: "To peace between man and computer." This is a good sentiment and a necessary one. He came to me several years ago to see the results of my writing classes at the University of Hamburg. For two years members of his department have participated in my classes and have gained insights into old and new aesthetic experiences. The aim is to introduce these concepts into the rational and objective world of digital computers. A rare occurence, but a hopeful one.

After a visit to an exhibition of my students' works, Erwin Steen, production manager of the German publishing company, Rowohlt, made it possible for his staff and interested members of other departments of the firm to participate in my classes for half a year. This is another example of a positive reaction that can lead to deeper understanding of form and validity.
These events stand at the beginning of my reflections on technological developments of digital writing forms and production techniques at large publishing houses such as Rowohlt. I want to make it clear that I am not opposed to the changes that have been initiated by the electronic age, since I have witnessed how sensibly they can be dealt with.

After five centuries Gutenberg is being replaced by electronic data processing. The shapes of different alphabets that developed during this time are stored in memory through scanners or manual digitalization. Sophisticated processes can produce letters that rival handcut metal type in appearance. The quality of the output is of course dependent on the equipment and, even more important, on the programmers and their training.

Gutenberg's invention of movable type opened the door to mass production of texts in which handwriting was the norm. The most gifted writers in Europe dedicated themselves to the challenge and developed the outstanding type of their time. Typesetting was an elaboration of the art of handwriting. Metal type was and is the medium.

What has happened to writing since the age of the computer dawned on us? Nothing much. The canon of form and shape that grew and developed during the last five hundred years is constantly being recycled. There are, of course, some specialists at work in the studios, and they craft superior products. Sadly, however, most designers go around in circles, trapped in endless repetition. Their leitmotiv might well be Figaro's famous aria from Rossini's "Barber of Seville," "Garamond here, Garamond there . . . "

An equally sad topic are the thesaurus-like collections of alphabets that circulate among advertising agencies and typographers. The monstrosities that escape from between their pages can be viewed daily in our newspapers and magazines. Some of them bore us to tears, others surprise us with what can only be described as exhibitionism.

These are the two factors that are responsible for the state of the writing art: the decay of education on the subject in our schools and the digitalization of letters that turns variation into repetition.

Uses for new technologies in writing range from transfer type to home computers. Pitfalls are abundant. While teachers of basic script are paralyzed by endless arguments about methods and theories, industrial typesetters, printers, and producers of writing materials show growing awareness of the obligations.

"To perceive the writing itself, not just the information that it confers." Eckehard Schumacher Gebler, *Die Zeit* 4/26/85

The impulse for change must come from the ranks of management. If the loss of aesthetic quality is to be stopped, it will not suffice to improve machines. We have to focus on the product. This can only happen when training of all involved workers is upgraded considerably and when the almost forgotten knowledge of earlier typesetters is integrated into *new* technological developments.

Competent writers and designers can provide the link between Gutenberg's legacy and changing techniques. With care they can lead the way to a new aesthetic quality.

The demands of industry are high. It is imperative that we reevaluate the position of writing in the greater context of our European culture. Theoretical and practical studies of writing have to be integrated into the curricula of institutes of higher learning.

II

An Invitation to Fantasy
*and an Encounter
with Italic Writing*

Over the course of several decades I have observed high school graduates and found that after thirteen years of instruction, they knew nothing about the history of writing in the west or the development of our alphabet. They were exposed only to the mediocre script taught in our schools.

I do not know of a single book that is well made and carefully planned to teach young people about beautiful letters and encourage fantasy in writing. No attempt is made to create passion for practice. After four years of elementary education any sort of instruction in handwriting ceases completely. As a result, aesthetic values are neglected as we can plainly see, and the hundred symbols of our writing are barely *mastered* by anyone.

My main goal is to free my students from indifference and ugliness caused by incompetent previous instruction.

To master the art of writing is a joyful process. I tell my students that their natural sensibilities towards it have been buried rather than furthered, and I choose rhythmical patterns with no inherent meaning for first exercises. From skill comes pleasure. How these skills are unfolded is the topic of this book.

Abbreviations
A: *Evening class*
G: *Guest student*
S: *Student*
NN: *Name unknown*

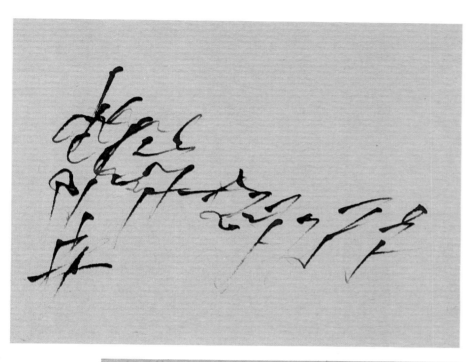

Any object at all can be used to draw fantastically abstract forms. We accumulate a collection of peculiar writing implements, such as leaves, reeds, quills, twigs, stones, shells, wood and metal shavings, strips of cardboard, wire loops, paper clips, plastic disks, matches, toothpicks, aluminum foil and plastic wrap, glass and earthenware shards, nails, knives, wires, strings, and ribbons.

We use black drawing ink (preferably not the cheapest kind: inks with a finer consistency will produce clearer lines and a better modulation), and we write on simple, smooth wrapping paper.

HEIKE PETERSEN *S*

BODO KAEMMLE *(Ikarus)*

VOLKMAR DÖRING *S*

Next I ask my students to forget everything they have learned before about writing and to just dip their utensil into ink and freely improvise rhythms on paper. No schematic repetitions or systems are wanted.
The impulse to invent new forms never fails to stimulate activity.

Phonetic symbols are meaningful constants. Rhythmical signs, by contrast, evolve from the subconscious mind in quick succession, intuitively and ever changing.

Sensations are transferred through arm, hand, and fingers, and through the tools that the hand moves onto the writing surface. Rhythm, a phenomenon of the mind, moves hand and tool and manifests itself in the world of objects.

Those rhythmical signs, originated from intuitions, made visible by a pen, convey no meaning, yet they are symbols for emotions and carry this information from the writer to the reader.
In writing these signs, sensibilities are awakened, the mind focuses on meditation, reflection, and self-consciousness.

Volkmar Döring .S

Sabine Vernimb .S

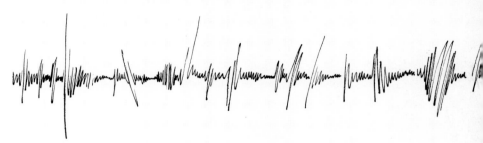

Sabine Vernimb .S

Volkmar Döring .S

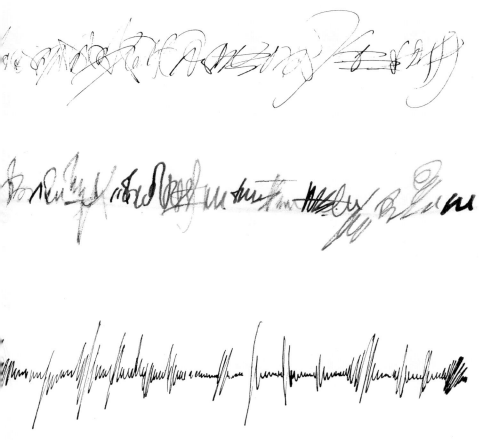

VOLKMAR DÖRING S

To reach this contemplative state of mind preparations are necessary. The possibilities range from listening to music, singing, or even screaming to body movements. Students are usually eager to experiment with those suggestions and can hardly wait to see the results.

Special attention should be paid to breathing techniques. Both writing and breathing are rhythmical activities and should be coordinated. Breathing audibly involves the ear and provides helpful feedback.

In the early stages of instruction it is important not to make changes in the familiar field of vision.

A regular-size sheet of paper should be used while eye and hand strive for a high quality of form.

It is only natural that students often find it extremely difficult to disregard what they have been taught before.

Christiane Hoffmann .S

Bodo Kaemmle .S

Christiane Hoffmann .S

KAREN HEHNKE S

Continuous progress towards truly aesthetic forms can be encouraged if the teacher suggests possible solutions to problems in a "hands on" approach.

CENGIS TALINLI S (TURKEY)

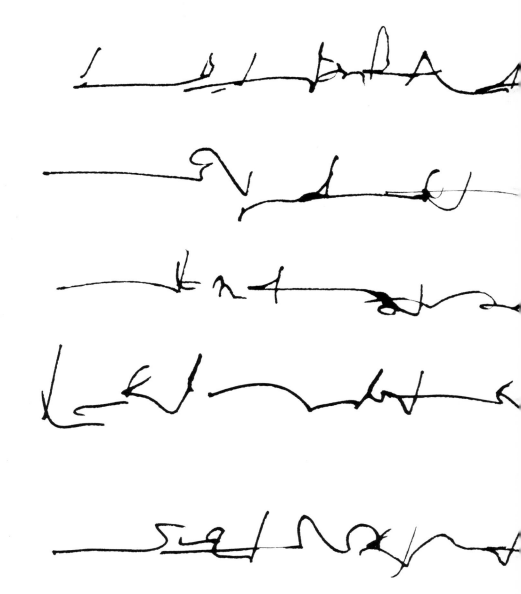

CENGIS TALINLI *S* (TURKEY)

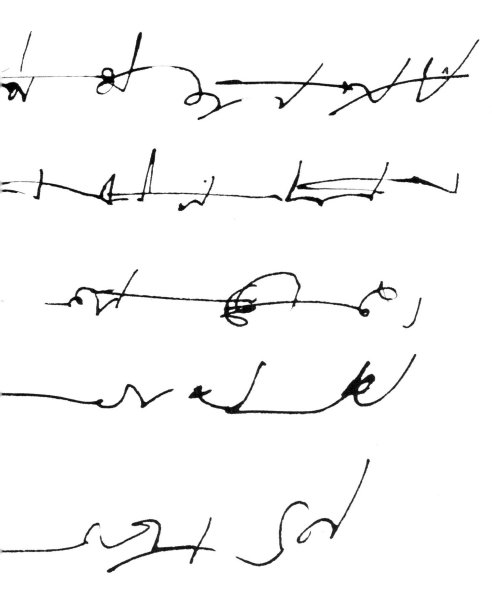

Dagmar Fitz S

VOLKMAR DÖRING 8

Early on it becomes obvious that the marks are not necessarily arranged in lines. Units of structures and modulations of tone start to appear.

DAGMAR WEDE S

When individual capabilities start to unfold, I urge the students to concentrate on single units of their work. This shift intensifies their efforts. To keep everything well in view, we use paper that is approximately 8 1/2 by 11 inches in size and restrict each character to about 2 by 3 inches.

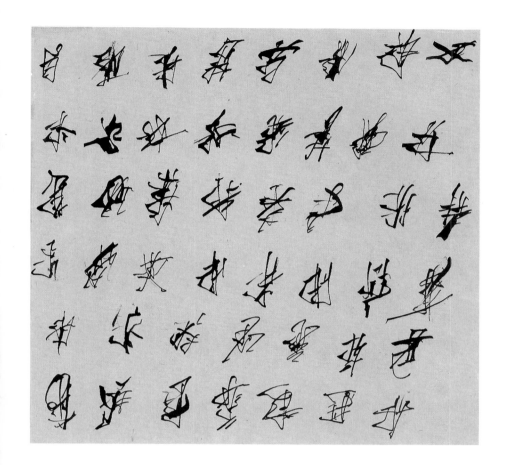

GESINE ENGLERT .S

FRANK J. SUHR .S

24

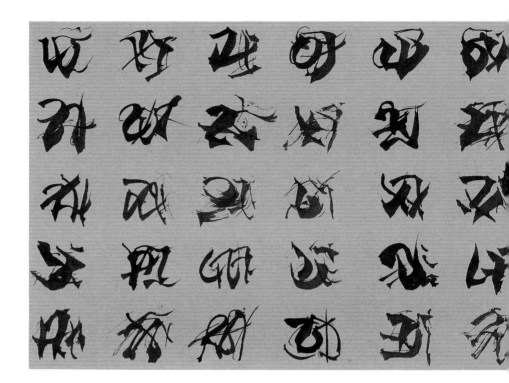

NOBERT TANZ S

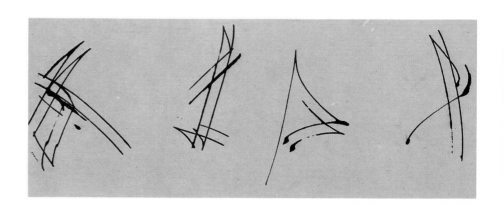

NN

STEFANIE SIEKKÖTTER S

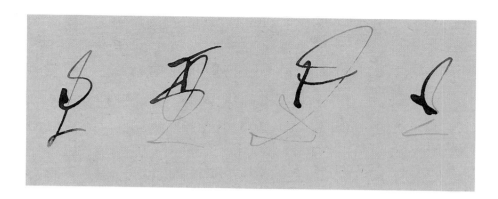

NN

FRANK J. SUHR S

RALF HOLZMÜLLER S

NN

GESINE ENGLERT S

Angela Arndt *S*

Stefanie Becker *S*

NN

H. Müller *S*

Heike Petersen *S*

Konstantin Richter *S*

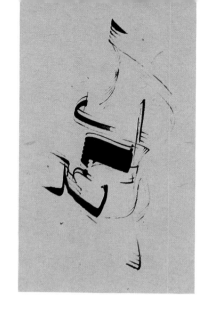

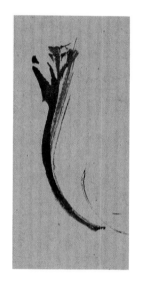

ELLEN STURM S

RALF HOLZMÜLLER S

ELKE ENNS *(Rowohlt)*

LAURENS THURN S

NN

KONSTANTIN RICHTER S

BÄRBEL BIWALD S

During the second work phase we vary the writing surface. White paper contrasts with watercolors of the finest consistency and causes heightened awareness and an even greater care in the use of the materials.

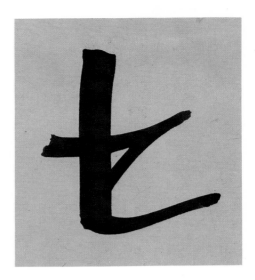

BÄRBEL BIWALD *S*

ANJA THOMSEN *S*

ANTONIA WIEFELSPÜTZ *S*

BRIGITTE NEUMANN *(Rowohlt)*

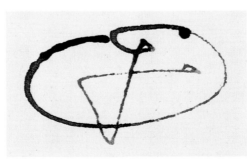

LAURENS THURN *S*

Frank J. Suhr *S*

Brigitte Neumann *(Rowohlt)*

Antonia Wiefelspütz *S*

NN

The separation from the shapes of well-known letters is a very difficult one. Similarities crop up again and again.

SIGRID ENGELMANN *(Ikarus)*

RENATE SUBEI *S*

URSULA PEIN *S*

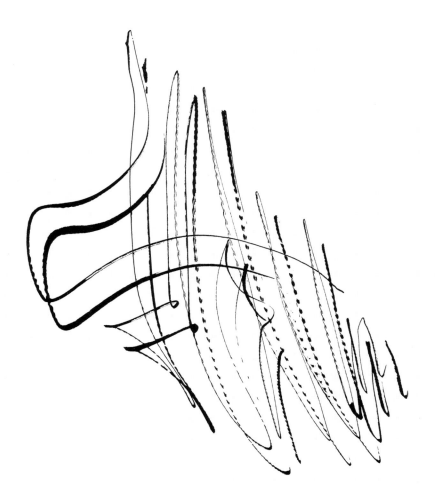

We study the written forms carefully to sharpen awareness of the process that transfers the idea to the paper. Intuitive movements and an improving sense of forms will lead to heightened awareness. The student who hones his skills on these exercises will be able to apply them to the study of historical alphabets.

BIRGIT HALGMANN S

Gertraud Baudy *S*

Angela Arndt *S*

Smadar Raveh *S* (Israel)

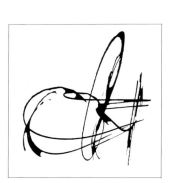

Dirk Messer *S*

Ute Martens *S*

Katjenka Krause *S*

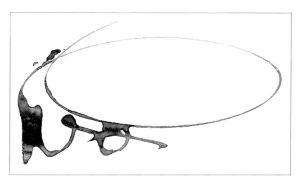

Kerstin Hauswaldt *S*

Kerstin Hauswaldt *S*

NN

BIRGIT SCHMIDT *S*

MARNIE MOLDENHAUER *S*

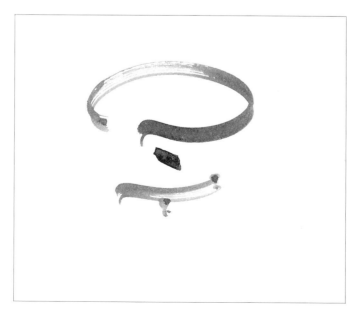

SOPHIE BUSCH *S*

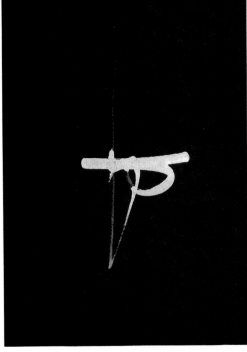

MARLIES FALLER *S*

KAREN HEHNKE *S*

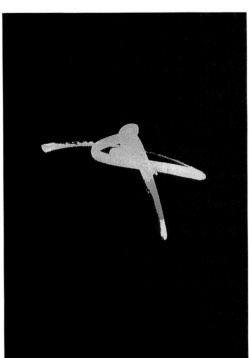

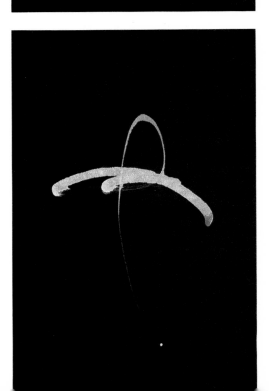

CLAUDIA MARTELLI *S* (ITALY)

SMADAR RAVEH *S* (ISRAEL)

NOBERT TANZ *S*

STEFANIE SIEKKÖTTER S

SMADAR RAVEH S (ISRAEL)

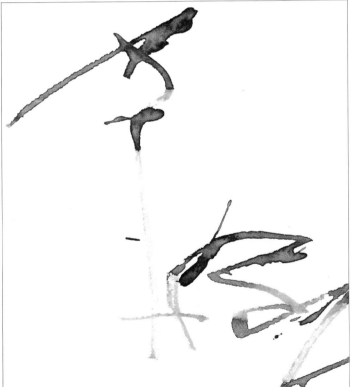

NN

37

MARGIT GRIESBACH *(Rowohlt)*

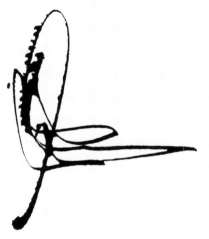

URSULA RADTKE *(Rowohlt)*

BIRGIT SCHMIDT *S*

ULF MATTHES *S*

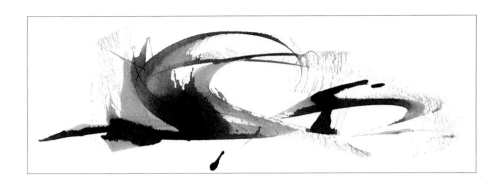

BIRTE KÖHN *S*

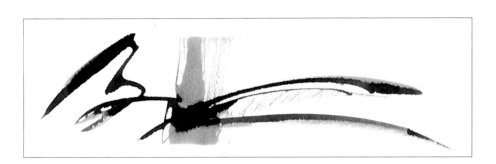

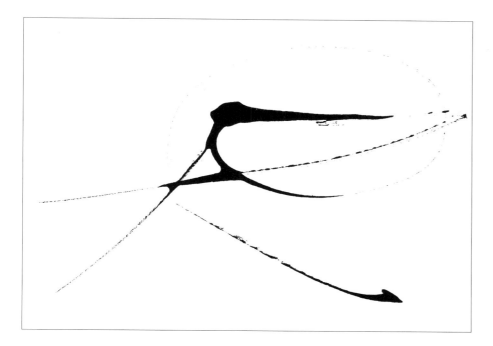

BÄRBEL BIWALD *S*

ECKARDT KLOOS *(Rowohlt)*

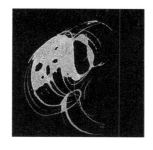

UTE MARTENS *S*

STEFANIE BECKER *S*

UTE MARTENS *S*

DIRK MESSER *S*

Stefanie Becker *S*

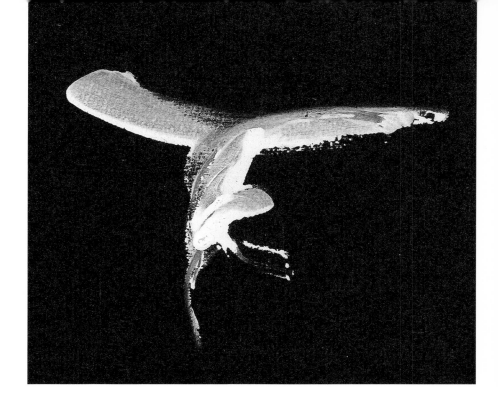

Dirk Messer *S*

Marnie Moldenhauer *S*

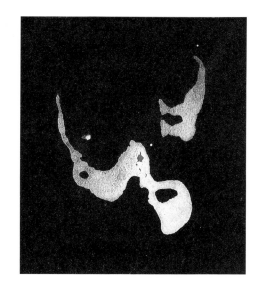

BODO KAEMMLE *(Ikarus)*

RITA CORDES *S*

Karin Peinert *S*

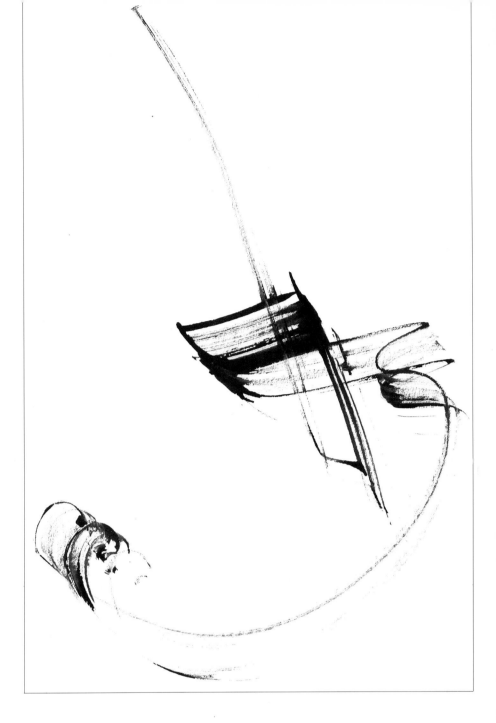

Cengis Talinli *S* (Turkey)

Sigrid Engelmann *(Ikarus)*

Andrea Duetsch S

Andrea Duetsch S

Ute Martens S

Gertraud Baudy S

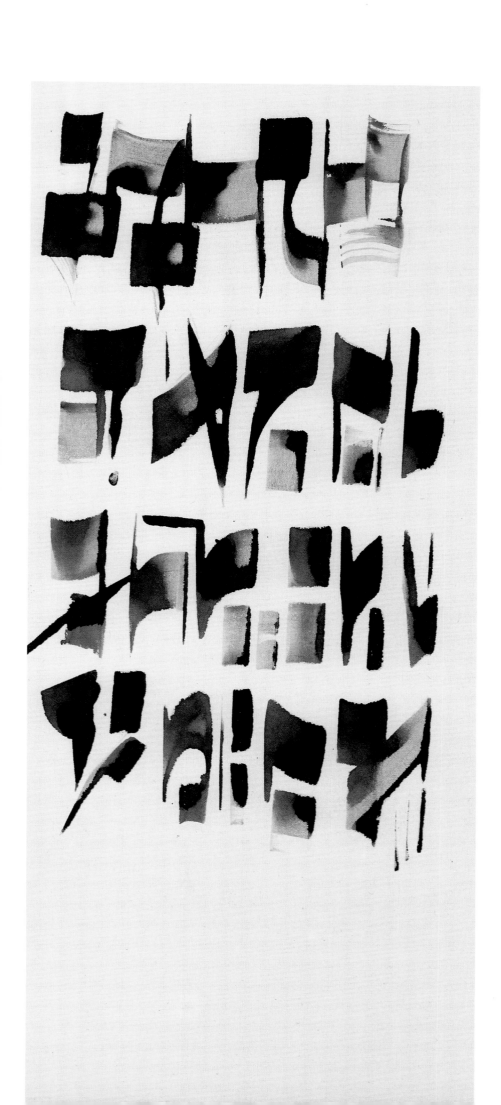

We start to compose our
marks onto a page of free
format. The focal point
still is the single character.

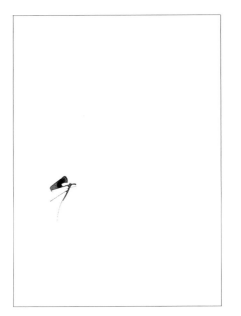

YVONNE BAGSTEDT *S*

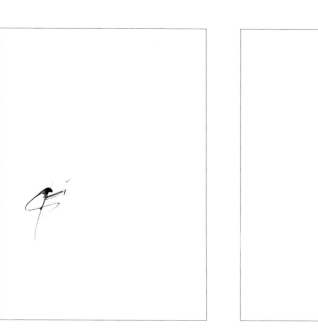

KIRSTEN SIEDENBURG-EVERS S

YVONNE BAGSTEDT S

The introductory period of play and experiments is concluded by the use of color and the choice of writing tools that create expressive structures. The rhythmical, contentless marks appear concentrated into abstract pictures.

Anneliese Hansen *(Rowohlt)*

Karin Iserloth *(Ikarus)*

SYBILLE BRUNNER *(Ikarus)*

FRANK J. SUHR S

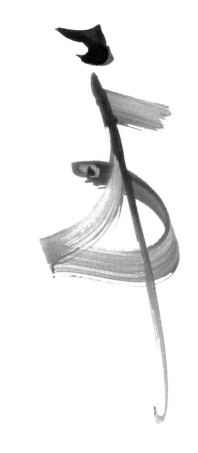

KARIN PEINERT S

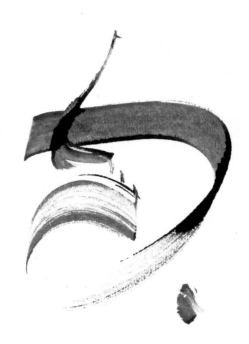

BARBARA NEINASS *(Rowohlt)*

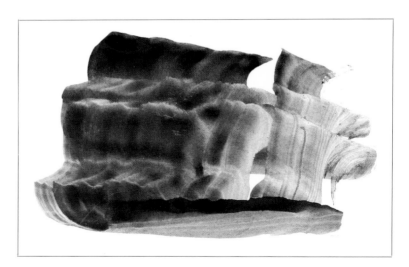

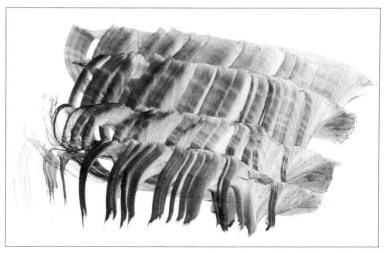

EDITH LACKMANN *(Rowohlt)*

SABINE KARA *(Ikarus)*

ELKE ENNS *(Rowohlt)*

Armgart Gross *G*

Sybille Brunner *(Ikarus)*

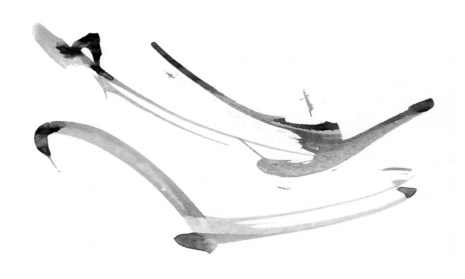

Helga Jörgensen *(Ikarus)*

Heide Hensel *(Rowohlt)*

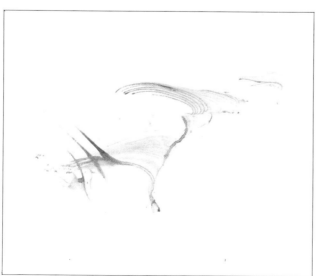

Uta Reitz *(Rowohlt)*

Anneliese Hansen *(Rowohlt)*

Marita Skawran *(Ikarus)*

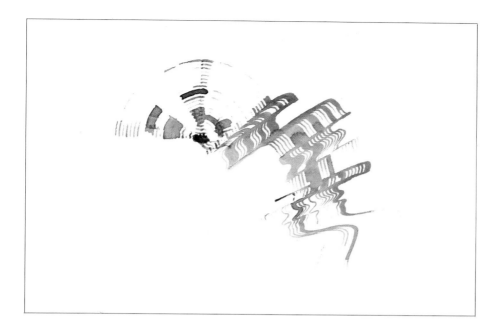

Sabine Kara *(Ikarus)*

NN

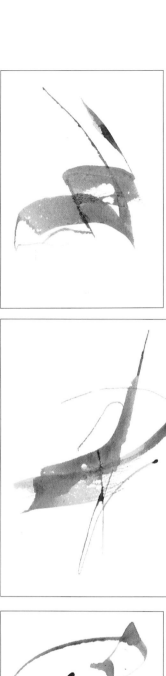

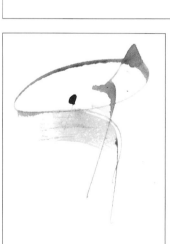

Ruth Freytag *S*

Ina Rafeiner S

DIRK MESSER *S*

DIRK MESSER *S*

MICHAEL KLAACH *S*

BODO KAEMMLE *(Ikarus)*

NN

CAY FIEHN *S*

JÖRG GRÖGER *S*

RICA LINDERS *S*

BÄRBEL BIWALD *S*

JULIANE GARSTKE S

DIRK MESSER S

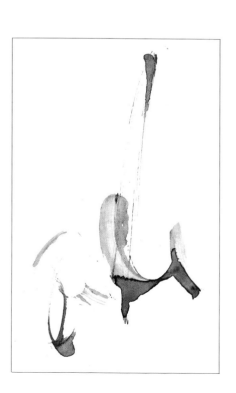

Susanne Adamek S

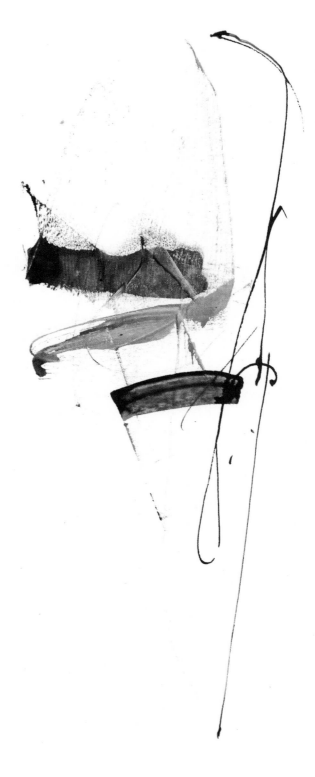

Rita Cordes *S*

F. Seifert *S*

NN

NN

NN

Towards the end of this stage, forms are carefully thought out and reduced.

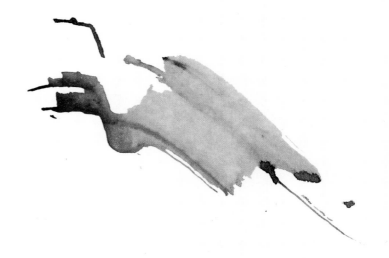

BIRGIT REINHART *S*

Iris Brandes *S*

Iris Brandes *S*

Birgit Reinhart *S*

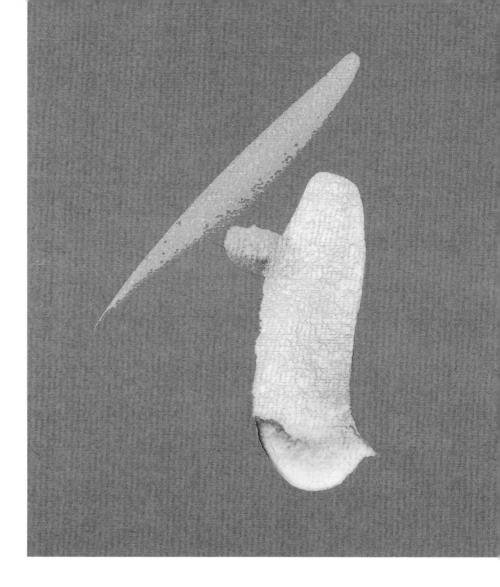

Ingrid Schade *S*

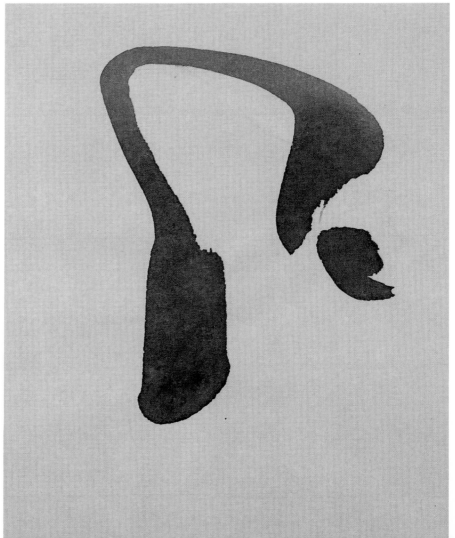

The visible shapes of the European phonetic alphabet have existed in almost unchanged form for more than two thousand years. During that time we consider the emergence of majuscules and minuscules particularly important steps in the development. Their forms remain constant but they contain countless variations of rhythm and harmony. Herein lies the creative aspect of writing. The surrounding cultural phenomena always influenced the rich diversity of forms.

"Solid workmanship and a knowledge of all organic growth are the foundations that allow unconscious creating to rise to the level of a work of art."

WALTER TIEMAN

In the first phase we concentrate on rhythm but we disregard established phonetic signs. The objects of our work carry no meaning; they are dictated and invented by the writers' rhythms.

In the second phase the students are introduced to theoretical and practical studies of italic writing, also known as cancelleresca or chancery script. This script has been in use since its inception in fifteenth-century Italy. The Renaissance shaped its lively forms, but we see no national influences.

DIETRICH MOHR *(Rowohlt)*

BRIGITTE NEUMANN *(Rowohlt)*

NN

Bewundert viel und viel gescholten 'Helena · · · Wenige Bücher stehen in einem so schlechten Ruf – wenige sind so viel
gelesen wie das Dekameron · Gelesen · Wer hat denn dieses Buch gelesen · Wer von den Zahllosen 'die es in die Hand
nahmen 'hat bei dem ersten Satz angefangen 'um beim letzten aufzuhören · Aber ist das nötig · Sagt nicht Boccaccio selber
selbst in seinem Nachwort : Wer diese Geschichten lesen will 'soll die lassen 'die ihm zuwider sind 'und die lesen · die
ihn freuen · Gibt es einen roten Faden 'der diese hundert verschiedenen Erzählungen verbindet · Es gibt einen · Und nur
wer diesen Faden sucht 'wird das Dekameron vollends verstehen · nur wenn er ihn gefunden hat 'darf sich ein Urteil
über den künstlerischen und den sittlichen Wert dieses Buches erlauben · Deshalb kann eine Einleitung in die Erzählungen
der zehn Tage nur ein Versuch sein 'den Platz zu bestimmen 'den das Buch als Ganzes in der Literatur und in dem
Leben seines Dichters einnimmt 'ein Versuch 'den Leser zu veranlassen 'es als ein einheitliches Kunstwerk zu betrachten ·
es als Ganzes zu lesen

Eine Rahmenerzählung ist eine Form · Was w wir Form nennen 'ist immer eine Überwindung · Wenn wir den Naturlaut
zu Worten formen 'die Gedanken zu Sätzen 'die Worte zu rhythmischen und metrischen Reihen · so ist das immer
eine Art zu siegen 'eine dauerhafte Umordnung der Natur · Wie wir uns bauend 'die Schwerkraft unterwerfen · so tun
wir es im Schreiben mit dem Raum und der Zeit · Ordnen heißt überwinden : Da sprach Gott es werde Licht !
Und es ward Und es ward Licht · Und Gott sah 'daß das Licht gut war · Dann schied Gott das Licht
von der Finsternis ·

Was uns aber immer von neuem erstaunt 'rührt und zum Untersuchen reizt 'was uns zu gleicher Zeit selbstverständlich
und unerforschlich und unerfindlich erscheint 'ist die geschlossene Eigenheit des einmal Geordneten 'die Selbständigkeit einer
Form 'Sie entsteht aus unserem Sieg · Sooft ich meine holdseligen Damen 'sinnend betrachte 'wie mitleidig ihr alle
von Natur aus seid 'erkenne ich 'daß das gegenwärtige Werk nach eurem Urteile einen harten und traurigen
z Anfang haben wird 'weil es an seiner Stirn die schmerzliche Erinnerung an das vergangene große Sterben
erträgt 'das allgemein von jedem verflucht wird 'der es miterlebt oder davon erfahren hat · Aber ich will nicht
daß ihr euch dadurch vor dem Weiterlesen abschrecken lasset 'lasset lasset lasset 'in der Meinung 'ihr
werdet beim Lesen schier immer durch Seufzer und Tränen wandeln müssen · Dieser schreckliche Anfang
soll euch nichts anderes sein 'als was den Wanderern ein rauhes und steiles Gebirge ist 'hinter dem die
schönen schönste und anmutigste Ebene liegt 'die sie um so lieblicher dünket 'je beschwerlicher das Erklimmen
und Herabsteigen war · Und so wie sich an die äußerste Freude Freude der Schmerz schließt 'so wird auch
der Jammer von einer hinzutretenden Lust begrenzt 'Auf diese g kurze kur kurze Traurigkeit – kurz sage ich
ich 'weil sie nur wenige Zeilen einnimmt – folgt alsbald das das süße s süße Vergnügen 'das das ich
euch vorhin versprochen habe und das ihr vielleicht bei einem also beschaffenen Eingange ohne ausdrückliche
Ankündigung nicht erwartet hättet · Und wahrhaftig 'hätte ich euch auf eine anständige Art von einer anderen
Seite als über diesen also also rauhen Pfad dorthin 'wo ich wünsche 'führen können 'so hätte hätte ich's gerne
getan · weil ich wünsche · weil es aber ohne diese Erinnerung unmöglich wäre 'euch den I Anlaß darzulegen ·
warum das 'wo was später zu lesen sein wird 'geschehen ist · so gehe ich notgedrungen an diese Beschreibung ·
Ich sage also 'daß seit der heilbringenden Menschwerdung des Gottessohnes eintausenddreihundertund achtund
eintausenddreihundertundachtundvierzig Jahre verstrichen waren 'als in die herrliche Stadt Florenz 'die alle
italienischen) anderen italischen italisch italischen italischen Staedte an Schoenheit überragt 'die todbringende
Pest gekommen ist 'd o die 'entweder durch die Einwirkung der Him Himmelskoerper oder wegen unseres
schlechten Wand Wandels von dem gerechten Zorne Gottes zu unserer Besserung über die Sterblichen geschieht '
tiefe einer unzähligen Menge von Menschen beraubt und sich unaufhaltsam von Ort zu Ort vordringend
traurigem nach Westen verbreitet hat ·

Originalsize

iese Erinnerung unmöglich wäre' euch den I

wird 'geschehen ist ' so gehe ich notgedrungen

'en Menschwerdung des Gottessohnes eintausen

hre verstrichen waren' als in die herrliche Sta

tischen italischen Staedte an Schoenheit über

die Einwirkung der Him Himmelskoerper

en Zorne Gottes zu unserer Besserung über a

---

*I choose italic for the first
formal calligraphy lectures
because the preliminary
exercises with free form
seem to prepare hand and
eye for this script's complicated forms.*

*For the first time the stu-
dents are required to
guide their pens in specific
ways and shape letters.
We use pens with light-
weight round handles.
The nibs are steel; later
we use reeds and quill
pens.*

*We write on graph paper
of superior quality, later
on a light-colored paper
with a hard surface that
yields a line with clear
contours.*

RENATE SUBEL S

In a white porcelain bowl we prepare saturated solutions of watercolors. The best choices for writing are indigo, sepia, black, burnt sienna, and English red.

A new metal nib is covered with a protective layer of grease, which would repel water and has to be removed in the flame of a match. Instead of dipping the pen we apply the ink between the nib and the ink reservoir with a brush. This way the quantity of ink can be controlled in reference to the length of the line.

Gerrit Noordzij says in his book "The Stroke of the Pen" that letters are pure form and writing is rhythm. He continues, "During the writing process the tool — the pen — has a direct influence on the appearance of the line. Tools like punches, cutters, chisels, and similar implements do not. The predominance of writing implies the predominance of the pen. We are free to choose other utensils, but western script will always be defined by the western tool: the wide-nibbed pen."

He is referring to a nib that produces fine or wide lines depending on the direction of the stroke.

Steel nibs, sometimes adapted to low letter heights by filing, and reeds or quills seem best suited to italic. The latter are cut and prepared by the students.

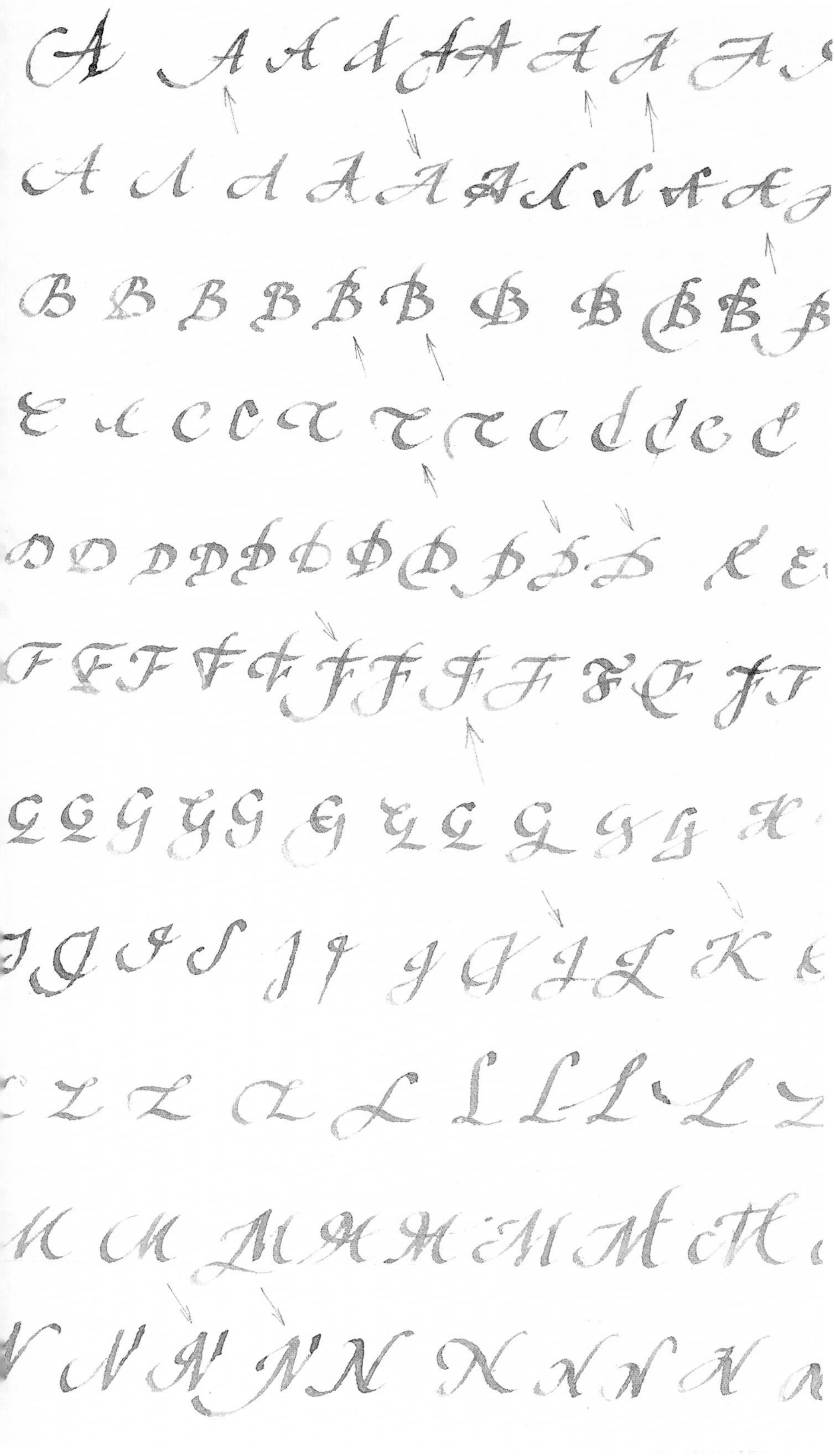

Left: NN

Kemal Zabtcioglu S (Turkey)

Sophie Busch S

Right: NN

Concentrated practice of single letters is followed by words and sentences. The aim is the emergence of an individual form codex.

SOPHIE BUSCH *S*

BODO KAEMMLE *(Ikarus)*

wherever loving hearts are found w

wherever loving hearts are found, it'

wherever loving hearts are found its Chr

I request no specific slant, but I discourage strict verticals or extreme italics.

...ri/tmastime the whole year round

...tmastime the whole year round

...time the whole year round

*Early on we see individualization. The student has to decide what is aesthetic and usable.
A critical exploration of historic examples is often helpful.*

rhododendron

rhododenron

R R R R

P P P P

A A A A

SIGRID ENGELMANN *(Ikarus)*

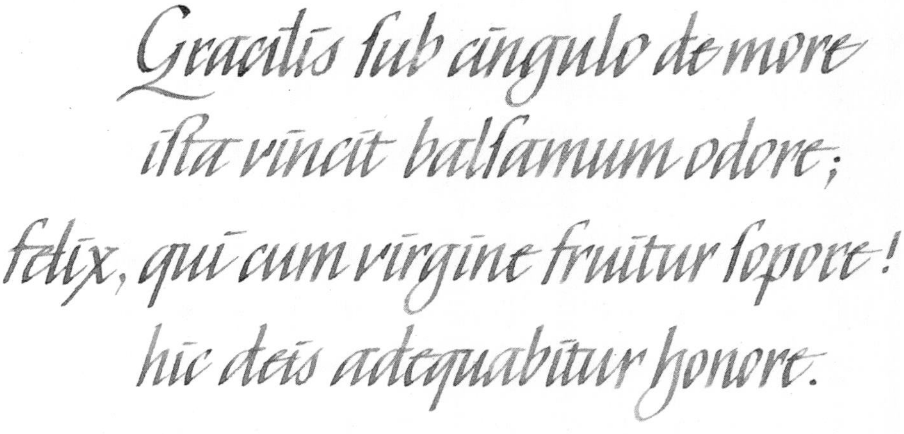

Gracilis sub angulo de more
ista vincit balsamum odore;
felix, qui cum virgine fruitur sopore!
hic deis adequabitur honore.

Farbe und Duft. Bedenke, daß der Weingeist alle Farben und Düfte in sich aufnimmt, und wenn du Blau herstellen willst, so lege Kornblumen hinein, und für Rot Klatschmohn.

Rezept für Fleischfarbe in Glas. Um Fleischrot in Glas zu machen, nimm Rubine von Rocca Nera oder Granate und setze Milchweiß bottino zu. Auch armenischer Bolus ist gut zu gebrauchen.

Herstellung von Grün und Blau. Kupfergrün mit Aloe oder Galle oder Kurkuma gibt ein schönes Grün, auch Safran oder gebranntes Operment, aber ich bezweifle, ob es nicht binnen kurzem schwarz wird. Ultramarinblau und Glasgelb geben zusammen ein sehr schönes Grün für Fresko. Lack und Kupfergrün geben einen guten Schatten für Blau in Öl.

Von der zufälligen Farbe der Bäume. Die zufälligen Farben des Laubes der Bäume sind vier, nämlich Dunkel, Licht, Glanz und Transparenz.

Ecce florescunt arbore
ind tepescunt virgine
Paulcis a
Qui te caret hoc temp

Die Perspektive (lat. perspicere = deut[l]
das dreidimensionale Gegenstände in
Auges entsprechenden Weise darstellt.
Seherfahrungen müssen geometrische G

Der notwendige Überblick – Vorrausletzung
loren, wenn der Betrachter so nahe steht, da
denden Gegenstand voll überschauen kann.
gilt für das perspektivische Darstellen die
Objekt mindestens so groß sein soll wie die
weil weniger stark verkürzte Darstellung
so groß ist wie die größte Breite.

...sxtve canunt volucres:

...or !

...fit vilior.

...ichtig sehen) ist ein Abbildungsverfahren,
...ten Sehbedingungen des menschlichen
...r zeichnerischen Wiedergabe täglicher
...gesetze berücksichtigt werden.

...s perspektivische Darstellen – geht dann ver-
...ur noch durch Kopfbewegung den abzubil-
...abei entstehende Verzerrungen zu vermeiden,
...das der Abstand des Standpunktes zum
...Ausdehnung des Objektes. Eine bessere,
...steht, wenn der Abstand zwei- bis dreimal

Helga Jörgensen *(Ikarus)*

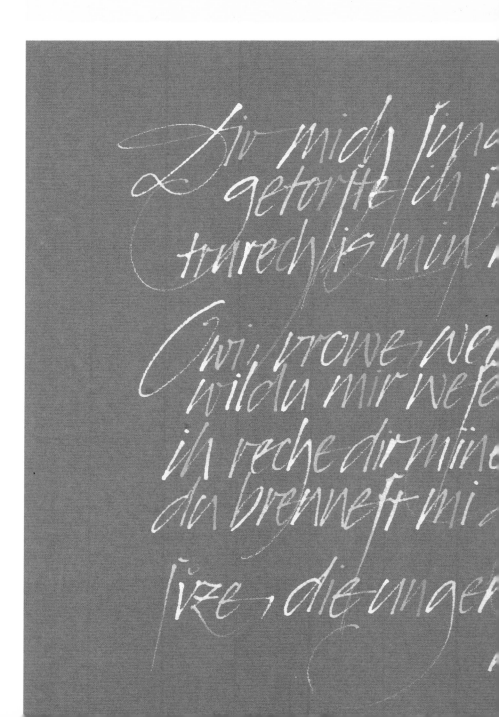

quiconque aura remarque les maux qui adviennt par
Inconsideration et temerité, celuy cognoistn facilement
les biens yprovient de bon et meur consil: et tout à
loyfr considera les affaires, en executant heureusement
tout les deliberations. Car c'est ne chose hazardeuse
de entreprendre que œuvre sans yprense meurement.

Ingrid Schade S

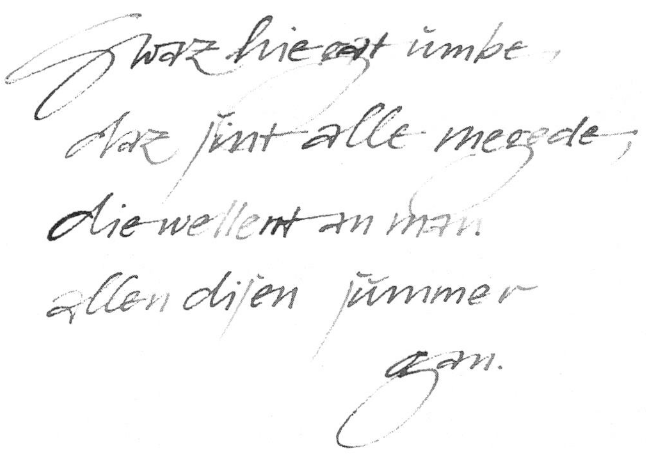

Swaz hie gat umbe,
daz sint alle megede;
die wellent an man
allen disen summer
gan.

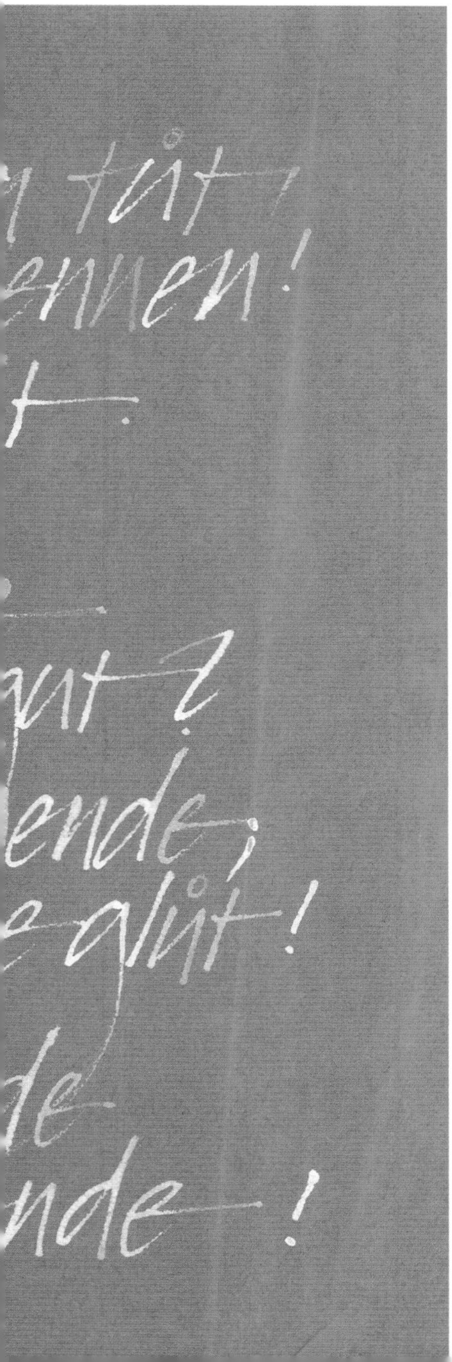

INGRID SCHADE S

Die Beschäftigung m

heutigene Menschen gle

Kindheit. Nur der

oder die der Naturvölk

schen als phantastische

Allegorien des M

Dichtung seit Jahrh

spielbar. Hermar

...ben, Sagen und Märchen ist hier der Geist der

...und mit der Pflege der Erinnerung und die eigene

...kultiviere vermag die mythischen Gebilde früher Zeiten

...billigen Überlegenheit des modernen Men-

...spinste abzutun. Ja man hat into sagen, daß mit dem

...Poesie an Gehalt verloren hat daß unsere

...schaft nur noch mit den Resten reicherer Zeiten ge-

...te meinem Brief. Sophie Busch im Juni 1986

William Shakespeare

Sonnets

To the onlie begetter of these insuing sonnets Mr. W. H.
all happinesse and that eternitie promised by our ever-
living poet wisheth the well-wishing adventurer in
setting forth.
                                        T. T.

I.

From fairest creatures we desire increase,
That thereby beauty's rose might never die,
But as the riper should by time decease,
His tender heir might bear his memory:
But thou contracted to thine own bright eyes,
Feed'st thy light's flame with self-substantial fuel,
Making a famine where abundance lies,
Thyself thy foe, to thy sweet self too cruel.
Thou that art now the world's fresh ornament
And only herald to the gaudy spring,
Within thine own bud buriest thy content
And, tender churl, makest waste in niggarding.
    Pity the world, or else this glutton be,
    To eat the world's due, by the grave and thee.

II.

When forty winters shall besiege thy brow
And dig deep trenches in thy beauty's field,
Thy youth's proud livery so gazed on now,
Will be a tatter'd weed, of small worth held:
Then being asked where all thy beauty lies,
Where all the treasure of thy lusty days,
To say, within thine own deep-sunken eyes,
Were an all-eating shame and thriftless praise.
How much more praise deserved thy beauty's use,
If thou couldst answer 'This fair child of mine
Shall sum my count and make my old excuse',
Proving his beauty by succession thine!
    This were to be new made when thou art old,
    And see thy blood warm when thou feel'st it cold.

III.

Look in thy glass, and tell the face thou viewest
Now is the time that face should form another,
Whose fresh repair if now thou not renewest,
Thou dost beguile the world, unbless some mother.
For where is she so fair whose unear'd womb
Disdains the tillage of thy husbandry?
Or who is he so fond will be the tomb
Of his self-love, to stop posterity?
Thou art thy mother's glass, and she in thee
Calls back the lovely April of her prime,
So thou through windows of thine age shalt see,
Despite of wrinkles, this thy golden time.
    But if thou live, remember'd not to be,
    Die single, and thine image dies with thee.

IV.

Unthrifty loveliness, why dost thou spend
Upon thyself thy beauty's legacy?

Nature's bequest gives nothing, but doth lend,
And being frank she lends to those are free:
Then, beauteous niggard, why dost thou abuse
The bounteous largess given thee to give?
Profitless usurer, why dost thou use
So great a sum of sums, yet canst not live?
For having traffic with thyself alone,
Thou of thyself thy sweet self dost deceive:
Then how, when Nature calls thee to be gone,
What acceptable audit canst thou leave?
    Thy unused beauty must be tombed with thee,
    Which used, lives th' executor to be.

V.

Those hours, that with gentle work did frame
The lovely gaze where every eye doth dwell,
Will play the tyrants to the very same
And that unfair which fairly doth excel,
For never-resting time leads summer on
To hideous winter, and confounds him there,
Sap check'd with frost, and lusty leaves quite gone,
Beauty o'ersnow'd and bareness every where:
Then, were not summer's distillation left,
A liquid prisoner pent in walls of glass,
Beauty's effect with beauty were bereft,
Nor it, nor no remembrance what it was:
    But flowers distill'd, though they with winter
    Leese but their show, their substance still lives sw

VI.

Then let not winter's ragged hand deface
In thee thy summer, ere thou be distill'd:
Make sweet some vial, treasure thou some place
With beauty's treasure, ere it be self-kill'd.
That use is not forbidden usury,
Which happies those that pay the willing loan,
That's for thyself to breed another thee,
Or ten times happier, be it ten for one,
Ten times thyself were happier than thou art,
If ten of thine ten times refigured thee:
    Then what could death do if thou shouldst depart
    Leaving thee living in posterity?
    Be not self-will'd, for thou art much too fair
    To be death's conquest and make worms thine

VII.

Lo! In the orient when the gracious light
Lifts up his burning head, each under eye
Doth homage to his new-appearing light,
Serving with looks his sacred majesty,
And having climb'd the steep-up heavenly hill,
Resembling strong youth in his middle age,
Yet mortal looks adore his beauty still,
Attending on his golden pilgrimage,
But when from highmost pitch, with weary car,
Like feeble age, he reeleth from the day,
The eyes, 'fore duteous, now converted are
From his low tract, and look another way:
    So thou, thyself outgoing in thy noon,
    Unlook'd on diest, unless thou get a son.

VIII.

Renate Fuhrmann S

Musíc to hear, why hear'st thou musíc sadly?
Sweets with sweets war not, joy delights in joy:
Why lov'st thou that which thou receiv'st not gladly,
Or else receiv'st with pleasure thine annoy?
If the true concord of well-tuned sounds,
By unions married, do offend thine ear,
They do but sweetly chíde thee, who confounds
In singleness the parts that thou should'st bear.
Mark how one string, sweet husband to another,
Strikes each in each by mutual ordering,
Resembling sire and child and happy mother,
Who, all in one, one pleasing note do síng:
    Whose speechless song, being many, seeming one,
    Sings this to thee: 'Thou single wilt prove none'.

IX.

Is it for fear to wet a widow's eye
That thou consum'st thyself in single life?
Ah! if thou issueless shalt hap to die,
The world will wail thee, like a makeless wife,
The world will be thy widow, and still weep
That thou no form of thee hast left behind,
When every private widow well may keep
By children's eyes her husband's shape in mind.
Look! what an unthrift in the world doth spend
Shifts but his place, for still the world enjoys it,
But beauty's waste hath in the world an end,
And kept unused the user so destroys it.
    No love toward others in that bosom sits
    That on himself such murderous shame commits.

X.

For shame! deny that thou bear'st love to any,
Who for thyself art so unprovident.
Grant, if thou wilt, thou art beloved of many,
But that thou none lov'st is most evident,
For thou art so possessed with murderous hate
That 'gainst thyself thou stick'st not to conspire,
Seeking that beauteous roof to ruinate
Which to repair should be thy chief desire.
O! change thy thought, that I may change my mind:
Shall hate be fairer lodged than gentle love?
Be, as thy presence is, gracious and kind,
Or to thyself at least kind-hearted prove:
    Make thee another self, for love of me,
    That beauty still may live in thine or thee.

XI.

As fast as thou shalt wane, so fast thou grow'st
In one of thine, from that which thou departest,
And that fresh blood which youngly thou bestow'st
Thou may'st call thine when thou from youth convertest.
Herein lives wisdom, beauty and increase,
Without this, folly, age and cold decay:
If all were minded so, the times should cease
And threescore year would make the world away.
Let those whom Nature hath not made for store,
Harsh, featureless and rude, barrenly perish:
Look, whom she best endow'd, she gave the more,
Which bounteous gift thou should'st in bounty cherish:
    She carved thee for her seal, and meant thereby
    Thou should'st print more, nor let that copy die.

Socrates, Glaucon, Polemarchos, Thrasymachos, Adein...
Cephalos

Summary

Book 1. Polemarchos invites Socrates and Glaucon to visit his father Cephalos' house. Various other friends are there as well. Cephalos talks about old age: eventually the conversation turns to the subject of justice. How do you define justice? asks Socrates. Polemarchos puts forward Simonides' definition -- to render what is due -- but this on examination proves unsatisfactory. Here Thrasymachos breaks in, maintaining that the whole conversation so far has consisted of nothing but pious platitudes. Justice, he says, is whatever suits the strongest best. Might is right. A ruler is always just. Socrates suggests that even a ruler sometimes makes a mistake, and orders his subjects to do something which is really not to his advantage at all. Is he just when he does this? Thrasymachos answers that in so far as he is mistaken he is not a true ruler. Socrates then argues that a doctor is primarily concerned to heal the sick, and only incidentally to make money: similarly, medicine seeks not its own advantage but the advantage of the human body. By analogy a ruler seeks the advantage of his subjects, not of himself.

Thrasymachos then rushes off on a new tack. Injustice, he says, is virtuous, and justice is vicious. Justice is everywhere at the mercy of injustice, which is reviled not because men fear to do it but because they fear to suffer it. Socrates sets out to disprove this view, and establishes that justice is apparently wise and virtuous, and at the same time more profitable than injustice. But, he says, he is still without a definition of justice.

Book 2. Glaucon and Adeimantos then develop further objections to Socrates' conclusions. Is justice, says Glaucon, any more than society's refuge from the consequences of the doctrine that true success depends on being as unjust as possible? Has it really a value for its own sake? Whereupon his brother Adeimantos adds that everybody is in fact as unjust as he can be without being found out; is there any value in justice itself, he asks, as distinct from a reputation for justice?

At this stage Socrates suggests that the nature of justice is more easily to be discovered in the macrocosm, the state, than in the microcosm, the individual. This is agreed and the discussion shifts to the origins and composition of a city-state. People associate for mutual support, because it is efficient: it enables each person to devote himself to the task he is best fitted for, and saves him from dispersing his energies in other tasks he is not fitted for at all, and which he will therefore perform indifferently. Socrates then describes the various classes of persons in a city, ending with the highest class, the rulers or guardians, who require the highest qualities. They must be both courageous and philosophical, both brave and wise.

How are these qualities to be developed?
This leads to the subject of education, which, Socrates seems to consist of gymnastic for the body and musik... the broad sense of the arts) for the soul. He takes literat... a part of musik, first of all, because education begins... says, in the nursery, with fables and fairy stories. These... st be very carefully censored to ensure a suitable moral... and in particular the gods must always appear in a... tuous light. God must be portrayed as the author of... good only, not of evil, and as incapable of falsehoo...

Book 3. Literature, Socrates continues, must de... only with suitable subjects, and only in a suitable... ner. He prescribes in some detail as to both subject a... form: in effect, the poet may tell only plain stories of... tuous people. The same considerations apply to musi... we mean the word: none but the Dorian and Phryg... the manly and sober modes, are to be allowed, and th... rhythms expressive of an orderly and brave life. The... ctice in the other arts is to be similarly regulated, an... the result a noble art, purified of unwholesomeness... extravagance, will develop in the young the characteri... ties of nobility. By learning to appreciate the good... the beautiful in art, they will learn to love them in...

In gymnastic, as in musik, a wholesome simpl... is prescribed. There will be in the city little disease and... lawsuits. But care must be taken to hold the balance... ween musik and gymnastic: excess in the former lead... effeminacy, and excess in the latter to hastiness. It is a... stake to suppose that musik trains the soul while gym... tic trains the body: gymnastic is as much a part of... soul's education as musik is, and the noblest natures... once brave and wise, require a harmonious blend of th... two.

From the noblest natures Socrates goes on, the rulers... city will be chosen - the best of the older men, selected fo... ir devotion to the state by various tests and carefully g... med for office. They will be assisted by the lower class o... ardians, the auxiliaries or soldiers. Their rule over the... will be supported by the mystical sanction of the myt... the three metals, gold, silver and iron. And they will... live the life of princes, but the simple life of soldiers, fre... from the distractions of wealth and luxury.

Book 4. Adeimantos remarks that the arrange... nts for the guardians do not sound very inviting. Soc... replies that this is not the point, even if it is a true cr... cism, which he doubts; he is concerned not with the ha... ness of parts but with one harmonious whole, the hap... city. The unity of this city, he says, depends mainly on... three principles - equal shares for all, so that there ar...

nd no poore, a physical limit of size, and the recogni
of merit regardless of birth. These precepts are to be
uarded by the educational system previously laid
1, and all else will then follow – a perfectly arran-
ty which will endure as long as the purity of the
n itself is maintained.

is the perfect city it must contain justice and be
wisdom, courage and temperance. Wisdom, says
tes, is to be found in the thinking element, the gu-
ns, and it is the knowledge in the light of which
ead the city. Courage or spirit, the quality of the sol
is the preserver of the constitution from the twin
ers of war and sedition. Temperance is common to
ree classes, and is the harmonious and beneficial re
ship between them. Now for justice – which is the
e that enables all the others to flourish, and in none
than the old principle put forward in Book 2, by
h each class does the work for wt which it is fitted wt
presuming upon the preserves of the others.

uch for the city. Applying this argument to the in-
dual, Socrates finds that the three classes in the state
flected in three elements in the soul, the reasoning, the
ted, and the desiring, corresponding to the counsell-
he assistants or soldiers, and the producers. Justice
refore the due arrangement of these three elements
eir proper stations in the soul, namely that the rea-
g part rules, with its auxiliary the spirited part,
the desiring part.

ates then begins to discuss the nature of injustice, and
ve types of political structure. One type, the only go
one, has been dealt with, the other four are all mo
less bad.

5)   Socrates is here interrupted by Polemar-
who asks him to fill in the outline of the perfect ci
more detail, before going on to the degenerate ones.
leads to a long digression, the main theme being pi
up again at the start of Book 8.

r a little preliminary skirmishining Socrates deals
the position of women in the perfect city. Woman,
ys, is the weaker sex, but there are no occupations
hich a woman is unfitted merely because she is a
an. He then describes a society in which all institu
s and relationships are ruthleßly subordinated to
reservation of the unity of the state, and private
s well as private property are rejected. The city-sta
is becomes the smallest as well as the largest – in fac
the only – unit of social life.

spirited, and the desir
ors, the assistants or so
is therefore the due arr
in their proper station
soning part rules, with
over the desiring part
Socrates then begins to
the five types of politic
good one, has been dea
re or less bad.

Book 5.)   Socrate
dos, who asks him to
ty in more detail, befor
This leads to a long dig

KARIN PEINERT S

abcdefgh
rſstuvw
ABCDE
LMNOPQR

Das größte ist das Alphabet, denn alle Weisheit
den Sinn, der's recht zusammenzusetze

presently my soul grew stronger

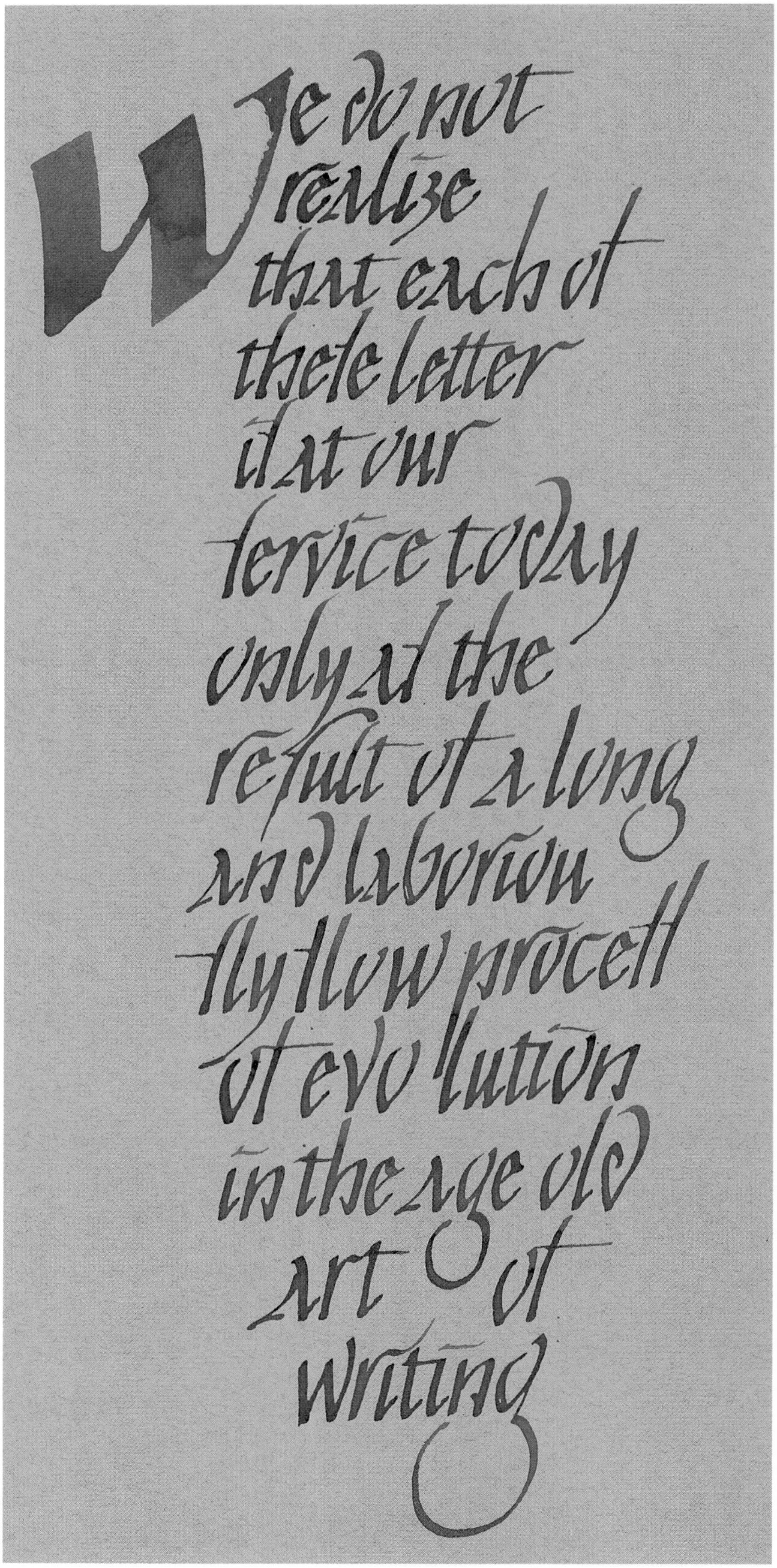

PETER PIATKE S

We do not
realize
that each of
these letter
that our

service today

only as the

result of a long

and laborious

ly slow process

of evolution

in the age old

art of

writing

HELGA JÖRGENSEN *(Ikarus)*

there
were
times   when all the world's asleep
the
questions
run too deep

NN

GÜNTER VORTISCH *A*

In 1920 Rudolf Koch created a landmark in the development from writing to calligraphy with his hand-printed text, "In the world ye shall have tribulation: but be of good cheer; I have overcome the world."

Expressive interpretation of texts through altered letters has opened a new dimension in writing. Even ugliness can be tolerated in this context. The works of Ernst Schneidler and his charming student Eva Aschoff are examples of this expressive style.

Nataly Mackensen S

"Handwriting is an independent expression of the author's character. We can convey sentiment, passion, direction, or melody through calligraphy. Reading an inscription can turn into an experience. To the calligrapher writing is much more than a vehicle for communication. It is capable of tenderness, of crying, and of rage. Within the simple shapes of script beats the pulse of life."

Oldrich Menhart

We choose words or phrases and explore their meaning. After a phonetic analysis we decide on a specific typeface. We contemplate how the interpretation of the words can be made visible.

Quality and validity can only be gained if practice with contentless rhythmical forms is combined with intensive studies of conventional forms. (An example is abstraction in art, which is not possible without previous exposure to nature studies.)

HEIDRUN BONNNET S

KARIN PEINERT S

I refer to this kind of writing as rhythmical forms with content. The letters with their inherent meaning are combined into a text. They are not, however, presented in their historic form, but evolve into an expressive new one.

If intuition and technical skills are sufficiently developed, emotions and feelings can be related to the viewer.

KARIN PEINERT S

We repeat this process
until a satisfying result is
achieved. Students fre-
quently produce dozens or
hundreds of versions.

The chosen one is en-
larged by means of a grid
onto a poster board to
show irregularities caused
by the pen or the paper.

The existing tonalities and
structures of the original
are introduced into the
enlargement with the help
of a lithography pen in a
pointillistic manner.

CHRISTIANE HOFFMANN S

LEONORE VON BENSFELD S

Jens Rademacher S

Heinz Waters S

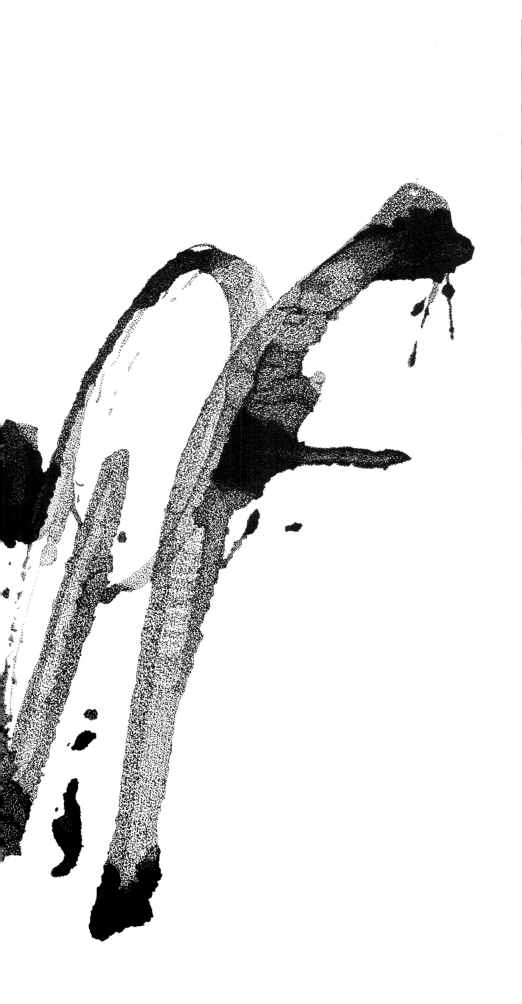

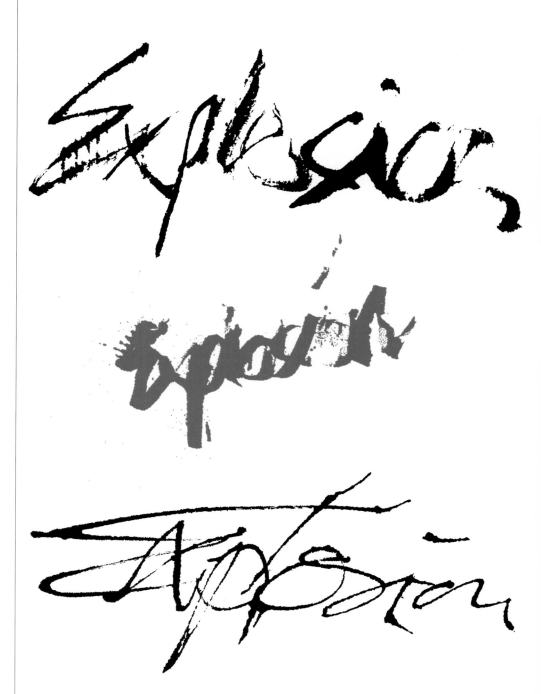

During the first semester fantasy and play create the fascination that makes intensive studies possible. Dexterity is gained, and we progress to the exacting task of studying the rich variety of aesthetic forms that were generated during the development of European writing.

The topic is the Roman letters that were the basis of western writing up to the time of the hand-drawn typefaces of the nineteenth century.

III

The Focal Point
ROMAN LETTERS

"Unfortunately we know nothing about the gifted originators of our scripts. Their names are lost in the darkness of antiquity like the names of the great ones that gave us the wheel, the bow and arrow, and the sail."

I. J. GELB

"Writing can only exist within the context of culture; culture cannot exist without writing."

I. J. GELB

CHRISTOPH MANNSHARDT S

DVM GERMINIA IMPERIVM
SVPERIOREM SVBACTA
CALORIA BACTVS INVISVS
TIBERI FINIOLEM XEYIINOBI
NEGLEBANT DOMINILTAS
OBSERVANT BOVTONI
BELLVM HOSTES AVGVSTVS
VESTVM IARIFARI RELEQVI
LEBERVRST TARQVIS SVPER
LEBENSIANG RELAXEN DORN
IMAVG GNMVMEST
XEROX HVMILITAS BELLVM
DI CVM TRIBVBIS ADORTI
SVNT VVLNERA DVM HOSTES
OSSA SVCCESIT EDVCABANDVR
NVCABANDI VERSATOX ZVLV
CONDARENT SVMA DORI
BARBAROS ET QVO TRISTIORES
CHRISTOPHERVS NIXBOCC
MAGNO SVPREMA ACERIM
YIIEFI TVLIVS FISCVS COMBO
TERRARVMEIVS SOLVENTI
TERTIA GERMANAI FOXTEM
CONSVLTARE LIMA ZOLEX

MARLIES KENDZIA S

ESTININSVLADEQVADIXIAEDESMINERVAE
QVAMMARCELLVSNONATTIGERAISEDPLE
NAMATQVEORNATAMRELIQVERATATAB
ISTOSICSPOLIATA ATQVEDIREPTAESTVTNON
ABHOSTEALIQVOQVIETIAMINBELLORELIGI
ONEMETIVSRETINERETSEDABARBARISPRAD
ONIBVSVEXATAESSEVIDEATVRPVGNAEQV
ESTRISAGATHOCLIREGISINTABVLISPRAEGL
AREPICTAERATHISAVTEMTABVLISPARIETES
INTERIORESAEDISVESTIBANDVRISTECVM
AEDEMILLAMIPOPTERDIVTVRNAMPACEM
FIDEMQVE FIDEMQVEPOPVLISYRACVSANI
SACRAMESSEAVDIVISSETOMNESEASTABVI
ASABSTVLITDICIETIAMPOTESTIVDICESISTV
MORNAMENTA MINERVAEVIRGINISIND
OMVMSVAMMERETRIGCIAMTRRANSTVI
ISSEVIGINTIETSEPTEMPRAETERATABVIAS
PVLCHERRINEPICTASEXEADEMAEDESVST
VLITINQVIB BVSERAERANTIMAGINESREGV
AASICILIAE.

ESTININSVLADEQVANVPER
DIXIAEDISMINERVAEQVAM
MARCCCELLVSNONATTIGER
ATSEDPLENAMATQVORNA
TAMARELIQVERATATABISTOS.

QVISFENESTRAMFRE
GERIT·INEAMEDIVMP
ARTEQVAMTERTIANI
INSIDENTFESTRAALI
QVAFRACTAESTVINI
ICVSTOSDOMVSIR
ATVSETMINACIVLVT
EDISCIPVLISQVAERI
TOVISHOCFICITTERI
IANTESSESIMVLANT
ITAQVECONCLAMEN
TCERTEALIQVISFICE
RITADQVATORDINA
RIVSMENOSGENVIT
DMAIORQVAEDMOR
ATIOBENETALISVIRT
PERICVLIVMISTVDI

We start with the three great roman scripts, quadrata, uncials, and rustic capitals. The dexterity that was achieved through studies of chancery script and the previous eye training becomes essential now.

BOHN-CHANG-KOO S (KOREA)

GRAVITATIONSWELLEN
DERGEKRVMMTERAVMDEHNTDIEOBIEKTEDVRCH
GEZEITENKRAEFTE·EINSTEINSTGRAVITATIONSW
ELLENSTRECKENDIEOBIEKTEINVERSCHEIDENENRI
CHTVNGEN·GRAVITATIONSWELLENSINDEXTREM
SCHWACH·HEFTIGEKOSMISCHEEREIGNISSESOLLTE
NENTDECKBAREGRAVITATIONSWELLENAVSSENDEN
GALILEISGEHEIMNIS
WIRKVNGENDERGRAVITATIONVNDDERBESCHLEVNI
GVNGSINDAEQVIVALENT·ALLESMVSSGLEICHSCHNELL
FALLEN·LICHTKRVEMMTSICHINEINEMBESCHLEVNIG
TENRAVMSCHIFF·EINBESCHLEVNIGTESRAVMSCHIFF
KOENNTEHINTERSICHEINSCHWARZESLOCHERZEV
GEN·DIEBEWEGVNGDESMONDESBESTAETIGTEINSTEI
NSAEQVIVALENCEPRINCIP
METHVSALEMIMRAVMSCHIF
BIOLOGISCHEVHRENVNDATOMVHRENLAVFENNIC
HTGEGENEINANDER·EINSCHWARZESLOCHZVBEO
BACHTENERHAELTIVNG·HOCHGESCWINDIGKEIT
SREISENERHALTENIVNG·DIESPEZIELLERELATIVITAE
TSTHEORIEBEHANDELTSCHNELLEBEWEGVNG·INST
ABILETEILCHENLEBENLANGERWENNSIESICHRACH
BEWEGEN
SCHIENENAMHIMMEL
VNANGETRIEBENEOBIEKTEREISENSOGERADEAVS
WIEESIMGEKRVEMMTENRAVMMOEGLICHIST·EINO

NANCY HUNTER S (CANADA)

Heidrun Bonnnet S

MAECENASATAVISEDITEREGIBVSOETPRAESIDIVMET
DVLCEDECVSMEVMSVNTQVOSCVRRICVLOPVLEI
OLYMPICVMCOLLEGISSEIVATMETAQVEFERVIDIS
EITATAROTISPALMAQVENOBILISTERRARVM
DOMINOSEHITADDEOSHVNCSIMOBILIVATVRI
QVIRITVMCERTATTERGEMISTOLLEREHONORIB
ILLVMSIPROPRIOCONDIDITHORREOQVIDQVIDDE
LIBYCISERRITVRAREISGAVDENTEMPATRIOS
FINDERESARCVLOAGROSATTALICISCONDICIONIBV
NVMQVAMDEMOEAS YTTRABECYPRIAMYRTOV
PALVSNAVTASECETMARELVCTANTEMICARIIS
ELVCTIBVSAFRICVMMERCATORMETVENSOTIVM
ETOPPIDILAVDATRVRASVIMOXREFICITRATES
QVASSASINDOCILISPAVPERIEMPATIESTQVINEC
ETERISPOCVLAMASSICINECPARTEMSOLIDO
DEMEREDEDIESPERNITNVNCIRIDIMEMBRASVB
ARBVTOSTRATVSNVNCADAQVAELENECAPVT
SACRAEMVLTOSCASTRAIVANTETLITVOTVBAE
PERMIXTVSSONITVSBELLAQVE
MATRIBVSDETESTATA MANETSVBIOEFRIGIDO
ENATORTENERAECONIVGISINMEMORSEVISA
ESTCATVLISCERAFIDELIBVSSEVRVPITTERETES
MARSVSAPERPLAGASMEDOCTARVMHEDERAE
PRAEMIAFRONTIVMDISMISCENTSVPERISME
GELIDVMNEMVSNYMPHARVMQVELESCVM
SATYRISCHORISECERNVNTPOPVLOSINEQVETIBI
EVTERPECOHIBETNECPOLYHYMNIALESBOVM
REFVGITTENDEREBARBITONQVODSIMELYRICIS
ATIBVSINSERESSVBLIMIFERIAMSERDERAERDIC
INTEGERITAESCELERISQVEPVRVSNONEGETMAVR
IACVLISNEQVEARCVNECENENATISGRAIDASAGITTI
FVSCEPHARETRASIEPERSYRTISITERAESTOVSASSIE
FACTVRVSPERINHOSPITALEMCAVCASVMELQVAELO
FABVLOSVSLAMBITHYDASPESNAMQVEMESILALYP
INSABINADVMMEAMCANTOLALAGANETVLTRA
TERMINVMCVRISOAGOREXPENDISFVGITINERMEM
QVALEPORTENTVMNIQVEMILITARISDAVNIASLATI
ALITAESCVLETISNECIVBAETELLVSGENERATLEONVA
ARIDANVTRIX

Jan von Hugo S

CATILINA

SENATV

NTRIBVLATIONIE
NVENERVNTNOS
OPTERCANONTI
SDVMTVRBABIT
AETTRANSFEREN
NTESINCORMAI
VERVNTETTVRB
AQVEEORVMCC
TISVNTMONTES
TVDINEEIVSFLVA
PETVSLETIFICAT
EMDEISANCTIFI
ABERNACVLVMA
TISSIMVSDEVSIN

FRANCOISE NIFLÉ *S* (FRANCE)

CATVLLVS CARM. CIX CX CXI CXII CXIII CXIV CXV

CIX

IOCVNDVM MI MEA VITA MIHI PROPONIS AMOREM
HVNC NOSTRVM INTER NOS PERPETVVMQVE FORE
DI MAGNI FACITE VT VERE PROMITTERE POSSIT
ATQVE ID SINCERE DICAT ET EX ANIMO
VT LICEAT NOBIS TOTA PERDVCERE VITA
AETERNVM HOC SANCTAE FOEDVS AMICITAE.

CX

AVFILENA BONAE SEMPER LAVDANTVR AMICAE
ACCIPIVNT PRETIVM QVAE FACERE INSTITVVNT.
TV QVOD PROMISTI MIHI QVOD MENTITA INIMICA ES.
QVOD NEC DAS ET FERS SAEPE FACIS FACINVS.
AVT FACERE INGENVAE EST AVT NON PROMISSE PVDICAE
AVFILENA FVIT: SED DATA CORRIPERE
FRAVDANDO EST FACINVS PLVS QVAM MERITRICIS AVARAE
QVAE SESE TOTO CORPORE PROSTITVIT.

CXI

AVFILENA VIRO CONTENTA VIVERE SOLO
NVPTARVM LAVS EST LAVDIBVS EXNIMIIS:
SED CVIVIS QVAMVIS POTIVS SVCCVMBERE PAR EST
QVAM MATREM FRATRES TE PARERE EX PATRVO.

CXII

MVLTVS HOMO ES NASO NEQVE TECVM MVLTVS HO
DESCENDIT: NASO MVLTVS ES ET PATHICVS. MO EST QVI

CXIII

CONSVLE POMPEIO PRIMVM ADVO CINNA SOLEBANT
MAECILIAM FACTO CONSVLE NVNC ITERVM
MANSERVNT DVO SED CREVERVNT MILIA IN VNVM
SINGVLA: FECVNDVM SEMEN ADVLTERIO!

CXIV

FIRMANVS SALTVS NON FALSO MENTVLA DIVES
FERTVR QVI TOT RES IN SE HABET EGREGIAS
AVCVPIVM OMNE GENVS PISCIS PRATA ARVA FERASQVE.
NEQVIQVAM: FRVCTVS SVMPTIBVS EXVPERAT.
QVARE CONCEDO SIT DIVES DVM OMNIA DESINT
SALTVM LAVDEMVS DVM MODO IPSE EGEAT.

CXV

MENTVLA HABET INSTAR TRIGINTA IVGERA PRATI
QVADRAGINTA ARVI: CETERA SVNT MARIA.
CVR NON DIVITIIS CROESVM SVPERARE POTIS SIT
VNO QVI IN SALTO TOT BONA POSSIDEAT
PRATA ARVA INGENTIS SILVAS SALTVSQVE PALVSDSQVE
VSQVE AD HVPERBOREOS ET MARE AD OCEANVM?
OMNIA MAGNA HAEC SVNT TAMEN IPSE EST MAXIMVS
VLTRO NON HOMO SED VERO MENTVLA MAGNA MINAX.

JAN VON HUGO *S*

Jens Rademacher S

COMMENTARIORVMBELLIGALLICILIBERSECVNDVS
CVMESSETCAESARINCITERIOREGALLIAINHIBERNISITAVTISVPRADEMONSTAVIMVSCR
EBRIADEVMRVMORESADFEREBANTVRLITTERISQVEITEMLABIENICERTIORFIEBAT
OMESBELGASQVAMTERTIAMESSEGALLIAEPARTEMDIXERAMVSCONTRAPOPVL
VMROMANVMCONIVRAREOBSIDESQVEINTERSEDARECONIVRANDIHASESSECAVSA
SPRIMVMQVODABNONNVLLISGALLISSOLLICITARENTVRPARTIMQVIVTGERMANO
SDIVTIVSINGALLIAVERSARINOLNERANTITAPOPVLIROMANIEXERCITVMHIEMA
REATQVEINVETERASCEREINGALLIAMOLESTEFEREBANTPARTIMQVIMOBILITAT
EETLEVITATEANIMINOVISIMPERIISSTVDEBANTABNONNVLLISETIAMQVODIN
GALLIAAPOTENTIORIBVSATQVEIISQVIADCONDVCENDOSHOMINESFACVLTATESH
ABEBANTVVLGOREGNAOCCVPABANTVRQVIMINVSFACILEEAMREMIMPERION
OSTROCONSEQVIPOTERANTHISNVNTIISLITTERISQVECOMMOTVSCAESARDVAS
LEGIONESINCITERIOREGALLIANOVASCONSCRIPSITETINEVNTEAESTATEINVLT
ERIOREMGALLIAMQVIDEDVCERETQVNTVMPEDIVMLEGATVMMISITIPSECVMP
RIMVMPABVLICOPIAESSEINCIPERETADEXERCITVMVENITDATNEGOTIVMSEN
ONIBVSRELIQVISQVEGALLISQVIFINITIMIBELGISERANTVTIEAQVAEAPVDEOSG
ERANTVRCOGNOSCANTSEQVEDEHISREBVSCERTIOREMFACIANTHICONSTAN
TEROMNESNVNTIAVERVNTMANVSCOGIEXERCITVMINVNVMLOCVMCONDV
CITVMVERODVBITANDVMNONEXISTIMAVITQVINADEOSPROFICISCERETVRREF
RVMENTARIAPROVISACASTRAMOVETDIEBVSQVECIRCITERXVADFINESBELGA
PERVENITEOCVMDEIMPROVISOCELERIVSQVEOMNIVMOPINIONEVENISSETREMIQ
VIPROXIMIGALLIABEXBELGISSVNTADEVMLEGATOSICCIVMBTANDECOMBOGIVM
PRIMOSCIVITATISMISERVNTQVIDISERENTSESVAQVEOMNIAINFIDEMATQVEPO
TESTATEMPOPVLIROMANIPERMITTERENEQVESECVMRELIQVISBELGISCONSENS
ISSENEQVECONTRAPOPVLVMROMANVMCONIVRASSEPARATOSQVEESSEETOBSID
ESDAREETIMPERATAFACEREETOPPIDISRECIPEREETFRVMENTOCETERISQVEREBVSI
VVARE

Jan von Hugo S

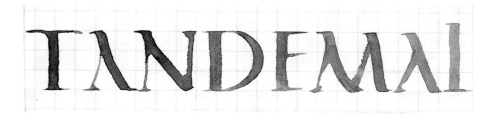

FRANCOISE NIFLÉ *S* (FRANCE)

NON TIBI OBIICIO QUOD HOMINEM
SPOLIASTI BENE AC SAPIENTER PC
MAJORES INSTITUERANT UT RE
RUM AGENDARUM ITA DICENDI
INITIUM A PRECATIONIBUS CA
PERE QUOD NIHIL RITE NIHILQUE
PROUIDENTER HOMINES SINE DE
ORUM IMMORTALIUM OPE CONSI
LIO HONORE AUSPICARENTUR. QU
I MOS CUI POTIUS QUAM CONSULIA

BENE AC SAPIENTER PC MAJORES I
TUERANT UT RERUM AGENDA
MITA DICENDI INITIUM A PRCA
NIBUS CAPERE QUOD NIHIL RITE I
ILQUE PROUIDENTER HOMINES
E DEORUM IMMORTALIUM OP
NSILIO HONORE AUSPICARENTUI
UI OMOS CUI POTIUS QUAM CONS
AUT QUANDO MAGIS USURPAN
SCOLENDUSQUE EST. ITAQUE A

TRIBUNI PLEBIS SUSPICIONIBUS
MAGIS QUAM ARGUMENTIS PE
CUNIAE CAPTAE RERUM ACCUSAR
UNT. FILIM CAPTUM SINE PRETIO
REDDITUM OMNIBUSQUE ALIIS REBU
S SCIPIONEM TAMQUAM IN EIUS U
NIUS MANU PAX ROMANA BELLU

MQUE ESSET AB ANTIOCHO CUI
TUM. DICTATOREM EUM CONS
ULI NON LEGATUM IN PROUINCI
A FUISSE NEC AD ALIAM REM EO
ROFECTUM QUAM UT ID QUOD IN
SPANIAE GALLIAE SICILIAE AFRICA
E IAM PRIDEM PERSUASUM ESSE

HOC GRACIAE ASIAEQUE ET O
BUS AD ORIENTEM UERSIS REGI
UE APPARERET: UNUM DOMI
NEM CAPUT COLUMENQUE IM
ROMANI ESSE SUB UMBRA SC
NIS CIUITATEM DOMINAM O
TERRARUM LATERE NUTLIM EN

TRIBUNI PLEBIS SUSPICIONIBUS
MAGIS QUAM ARGUMENTIS
PECUNIAE CAPTAE REUM ACCU
SARUNT. FILIUM CAPTUM SIN
E PRETIO REDDITUM OMNIBUSQ
UE ALIIS REBUS SCIPIONEM TAM
QUAM IN EIUS UNIUS MANU P
AX ROMANA BELLUMQUE ESSE
T AB ANTIOCHO CULTUM. DICTA
TOREM EUM CONSULI NON LE

CATUM IN PROUINCIA FUIS
SE NEC AD ALIAM REM EO PR
OFECTUM QUAM UT ID QUO
D HISPANIE GALLIAE SICILIA
E AFRICAE IAM PRIDEM PERS
USUM ESSET HOC GRACIAE A
SIAEQUE ET OMNIBUS ADO
RIENTEM UERSIS RGIBUS GE
NTIBUSQUE APPARERENT:
UNUM HOMINEM CAPUT

COLUMEN QUE IMPERII R
NI ESSE SUB UMBRA SCIP
SCIUITATEM DOMINAM
STERRARUM LATERE NU
MEIUS PRO DECRETIS PAT
N PRO POPULIS IUSSIS ESSE
XM A INTACTUM IUNIO,
U A POSSUNT URGENT. OP
ONIBUS IN NOCTEM PER
IS PRODICTA DIES EST. UI

TRIBUNI PLEBIS SUSPICIONIBUS MAGIS QUAM ARGUMENTIS PECUNIAE CAPTAE REUM ACCUS
T. FILIUM CAPTUM SINE PRETIO REDDITUM OMNIBUSQUE ALIIS REBUS SCIPIONEM TAC
AM IN EIUS UNIUS MANU PAX ROMANA BELLUMQUE ESSET AB ANTIOCHO CULTUM
CTATOREM EUM CONSULI NON LEGATUM IN PROUINCIA FUISSE NEC AD ALIAM R
EO PROFECTUM QUAM UT ID QUOD HISPANIAE GALLIAE SICILIAE AFRICAE IA
RIDEM PERSUASUM ESSET HOC GRACIAE ASIAEQUE ET OMNIBUS AD ORIENTE
RSIS REGIBUS GENTIBUSQUE APPARERET: UNUM HOMINEM CAPUT COLUMEN
E IMPERII ROMANI ESSE. INFAMIA INTACTUM INUIDIA QUA POSSUNT URGEN
RATIONIBUS IN NOCTEM PERDUCTIS PRODICTA DIES EST. UBI EA UENIT TRIBUN
ROSTRIS PRIMA LUCE CONSEDERUNT; CITATUS REUS MAGNO AMINE AMICORU
LIENTIUMQUE PER MEDIAM CONTIONEM AD ROSTRA SUBIIT SILENTIOQUE

TRIBUNI PLEBIS SUSPICIONIBUS MAGIS QUAM ARGUMENTIS PECUNIAE C
PTAE REUM ACCUSARUNT. FILIUM CAPTUM SINE PRETIO REDDITUM OMN
BUSQUE ALIIS REBUS SCIPIONEM TAMQUAM IN EIUS UNIUS MANU P
X ROMANA BELLUMQUE ESSET. AB ANTIOCHO CULTUM. DICTATOREM
M CONSULI NON LEGATUM IN PROUINTIA FUISSE NEC AD ALIAM RC
EO PROFECTUM QUAM UT ID QUOD HISPANIAE GALLIAE ASIAEQUE
OMNIBUS AD ORIENTEM UERSIS REGIBUS GENT

T. BÖNEMANN *S*

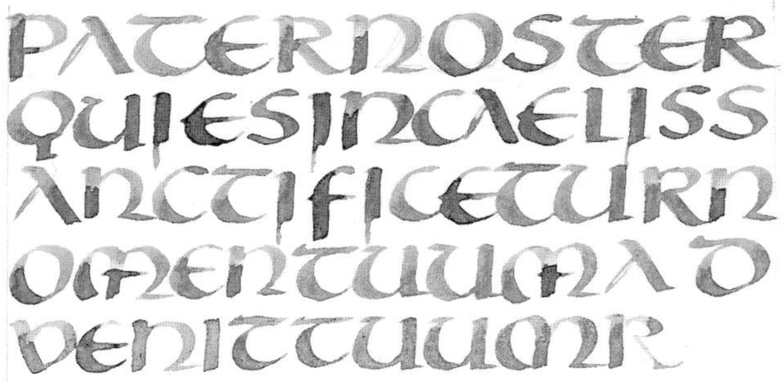

PATERNOSTER
QUIESINCAELISS
ANCTIFICETURN
OMENTUUMAD
VENITTUUMR

PATERNOSTER
QUIESINCAELISS
ANCTIFICETURN
OMENTUUMAD
VENIATREGNUM
TUUMFIATVOLU
NTASTUASICUTI
NCAELOETINTE
RRAPANEMNOS
TRUMQUOTIDIA
NUMDANOBISH
ODIEETDIMITT
ENOBISDEBITAN
OSTRASICUTET
NOSDIMITTIMU
SDEBITORIBUS N
OSTRISETNENO

ARMGART GROSS *G*

NN

GERTRAUD BAUDY S

GERTRAUD BAUDY S

DIE HARMONIE DER FARBEN   IOHANNES ITTEN

WER VON DER HARMONIE DER FARBEN SP
RICHT BEVRTEILT DAMIT DAS ZVSAMMENW
IRKEN VON ZWEI ODER MEHREREN FARBEND
IE ERFAHRVNGEN VND VERSVCHE VEBER SV
BIEKTIVE FARBAKKORDE ERGEBEN DAS VER
VERSCHIEDENE PERSONEN IN IHREM VRTEILVE
BER HARMONIE VND DISHARMONIE VERSCHIED
ENER ANSICHT SEIN KOENNEN MEISTENS WE
RDEN VON VIELEN FARBZVSAMMENSTELLVNG
EN ALS HARMONISCH BEZEICHNET DIE AHNLICH
E FARBCHARAKTER FODER GLEICHE TONWER
TE VERSCHIEDENER FARBEN ZEIGEN ES SIND DI
ES FARBEN DIE OHNE STARKE KONTRASTE NEBE
NEINANDER STEHEN IM ALLGEMEINEN BETREF
FEND IE AVSSAGEN HARMONISCH DISHARM
ONISCH NVR DEN GEFVELS BEZIRK ANGENEHM
NNANGENEM ODER SYMPATHISCH VNSYMPA
THISCH SOLCHE VRTEILE SIND PERSOENLICH
E MEINVNGEN OHNE OBIEKTIEVEN WERT DE
R BEGRIFF DER FARBEN HARMONIE MVSS AV
S DER SVBIEKTIV BEDINGTEN GEFVELSLAGE H
ER AVSGEHOBEN WERDEN IN EINE OBIEKTIVE
GESETZMAESSIGKEIT HARMONIE HEISST GL
EICHGEWICHTSYMMETRIE DER KRAEFTE DA
SS STVDIVM DER PHYSIOLOGISCHEN VORGANG
E BEIM FARBIGEN SEHEN BRINGT VNS DER LOES
VNG DES PROBLEMS NAEHER WENN WIR EINIGE
ZEIT EIN GRVENES QVADRAT BETRACHTEN VND
DANN DIE AVGEN SCHLIESSEN SO ERSCHEINT V
NS IM AVGE ALS NACHBILD EIN ROTES QVAD
RAT BETRACHTEN WIR EIN ROTES QVADRA
TSO SEHEN WIR ALS NACHBILD EIN GRVENE
S QVADRAT BETRACHTEN WIR DIESEN VERSV
CH WERDEN WIR FESTSTELLEN DASS ALS NAC

EIN AVSSERORDEN
TLICH WICHTIGE
GRVNDLAGE DER A
ESTHETISCHEN FA
RBENLEHRE IST DE
R FARBKREIS WIE E
R DIE FARBORDNV
NG DARSTELLT D
A DER FARBENKV
ENSTLER MIT FAR
BPIGMENTEN AR
BEITET MVSS SE
INE FARBORDNV
NG NACH DEN GESE
TZEN DER PIGMENT
AEREN FARBMISC
HVNGEN AVFGEBAV
T SEIN

DVRCH DIE DEFINI
TION DES HARMON
ISCHEN IST DER G
RVNDSTEIN GELEGT
FVER DIE HARMON
ISCHE FARBKOMPO
SITION

VM ALLE MOEGLIC
HEN HARMONIEEN
ZV FINDEN MVSS M
AN DIE MOEGLICH
EN ANORDNVNGEN IM
FARBKOERPER AVF
SVCHEN EE EINFACH
ER DIE ORDNVNG V
MSO EINLEVCHTE
NDER IST DIE HAR
MONIE

ZWEI ODER MEHR
FARBEN SIND DE HA
RMONISH WEN
NSIE ZVSAMMEN
GEMISCHT GRAV
ERGEBEN

GANZ ALLGEMEIN
KANN GESAGT WER
DEN DAS ALLE KOM
PLEMENTAEREN F

DE PROFVNDIS
SIQVARECORDANTIBENEFACTAPRIORA
VOLVPTASESTHOMINICVMSECOGITESS
EPIVMNECSANCTAMVIOLASSEFIDEM
NECFOEDERENVLLODIVVMADFALLEND
OSNVMINEABVSVMHOMINESMVLTAPA
RATAMANENTTVMINLONGAAETATECAT
VLFEEXHOCINGRATOGAVDIAMORETIBIN
AMQVAECVMQVEHOMINESBENECVIQVA
MAVTDICEREPOSSVNTAVTFACEREHAECA

DOMINICAPRIMAADVETV

INTROITVS
ADTELEVAVIANIMAMMEAMDEVSMEVSINTE
CONFIDONONERVBESCAMNEQVEIRRIDEANT
MEINIMICIMEIETENIMVNIVERSIQVITEEXSPEC
TABANTNONCONFIDENTVRVIASTVASDOMINE
DEMONSTRAMIHIETSEMITASDOCASTVASEDO
CEMEGLORIAPATRIETFILIOETSPIRITVISANCTISIC
VTERATINPRINCIPIOETNVNCETSEMPERETINSAE
CVLASAECVLORVMAMENETREPETITVR
    HICMODVSREPETENDIINTROITVMVSQVEADPS
ALMVMSERVATVRPERIOTVRANNVMNONDICIT
VRGLORIAINEXCELSISINMISSISDETEMPOREAB
HACDOMINICAVSQVEADVIGILIAMNATIVITATE
MDOMINIINCLVSIVE
ORATIO
EXCITAQVAESVMVSDOMINEPOTENTIAMTVAMET
TVENIVTABIMMINENTIBVSPECCATORVMNOSTROR
VMPERICVLISTEMERERIMVRPROTEGENTEERIPITELI
BERANTESALVNRIQVIVIVISETREGNAECVMDEO
PATREINVNITATESPIRITVSSANCTIDEVSPEROMN
IASAECVLASAECVLORVMAMEN

MISSALEROMANVMEDITIO

CYNTHIAPRIMASVISMISERVMMECEPITOCELLIS
CONTACTVMNVLLISANTECVPIDINIBVS
TVMMIHICONSTANTISDEIECITLVMINAFASTVS
ETCAPVTINPOSITISPRESSITAMORPEDIBVS
DONECMEDOCVITCASTASODISSEPVELLAS
IMPROBVSETNVLLOVIVERECONSILIO
EIMIHIIAMTOTOFVRORHICNONDEFICITANNO
CVMTAMENADVERSOSCOGORHABEREDEOS
MILANIONNVLLOSFVGIENDOTVLLABORES
SAEVITIAMDVRECONTVDITIASIDOS
NAMMODOPARTHENIISAMENSERRABATINANTRIS
IBATETHIRSVTASILLEVIDEREFERAS
ILLEETIAMHYLAEIPERCVSSVSVVLNERERAMI
SAVCIVSARCADIISRVPIBVSINGEMVIT
ERGOVELOCEMPOTVITDOMVISSEPVELLAM
TANTVMINAMOREPRECESETBENEFACTAVALEN
ILNMETARDVSAMORNONVLLASCOGITATARTES
NECMEMINITNOTASVTPRIVSREVIAS
ATVOSDEDVCTAEQVIBVSESTFALLACIALVNAE
ETLABORINMAGISSACRAPIAREFOCIS
ENAGEDVMDOMINAEMENTEMCONVERTITENOSTRA
ETFACITEILLAMEOPALLEATOREMAGIS
TVNCEGOCREDIDERIMVOBISETSIDERAETAMNES
POSSECYTAEINESDVCERECARMINIBVS
AVTVOSQVISEROLAPSVMREVOCATISAMICI
QVAERITENONSANIPECTORISAVXILIA
FORTITERETFERRVMSAEVOSPATIEMVREIGNES
SITMODOLIBERTASQVAEVELITIRALOQVI
FERTEPEREXTREMASGENTESETFERTEPERVNDAS
QVANONVLLAMEVMFEMINANORITITER
VOSREMANETEQVIBVSFACILIDEVSANNVITAVR
ESTISETINTVTOSEMPERAMOREPARES
INMENOSTRAVENVSNOCTESEXERCETAMARAS
ETNVLLOVACVVSTEMPOREDEFITAMOR
HOCMONEOVITAEMAIVMSVAQVEMIQVEMO
REIVRCVRANEQVEASSVETOMVTETAMOREHO
CVMQVODSIQVISMONITISTARDASADVERTERIT
VRESHEVREFERETQVANTOVERBADOLOREM
QVIDIVVATORNATOPROCEDEREVITACAPILLO
ELLENVESCOAVESTEMOVERESINVS
AVTQVIDORONTEAGRINESPERFVNDEREAVRA

PRO[P]
·ELEG

ENLIBER[
MONOBI[
PROP[

III·
LVM

PRIMVS

QVIDIVVATORNATOPROCEDEREVITACAPILLO
ETTENVESCOAVESTEMOVERESINVS
AVTQVIDORONTEACRINESPERFVNDEREMVRRA
TEQVEPEREGRINISVENDERECVLTV
NATVRAEQVEDECVSMERCATOPEDERECVLTVM
NECSINEREINPROPRIISMEMBRANITEREBON
ISCREDEMIHINONVLLATVAESTMEDICINAFIGVR
AENVDVSAMORFORMAENONAMATARTIFIC
EMASPICEQVOSSVMMITATHVMVSFORMOSACO
LORESVTVENIATHEDERESPONTESVAMELIVS
SVRGATETINSOLISFORMOSIVSARBVTVSANTRIS
ETSCIATINDOCILESCVRRERELVMPHAVIAS
LITORANATIVISPERSVADENTPICTALAPILLIS
ETVOLVCRESNVLLADVLCIVSARTECANVNT
NONSICLEVCIPPISSVCCENDITCASTORAPHOEBO
POLLVCEMCVLTVNONHILARASOROR
NONIDAECVPIDOQVONDAMDISCORDIAPHOEBO
EVENITPARTISFILIALITORIBVS
NECPHRYGIVMFALSOTRAXITCANDOREMARITVM
AVECTAEXTERNISHIPPODAMIAROTIS
SEDFACIESADERATNVLLISOBNOXIAGEMMIS
QVALISAPELLEISESTCOLORINTABVLIS
NONILLISSTVDIVMVVLGOCONQVIREREAMANTE
ILLISAMPLASATISFORMAPVDICITIA
NONEGONVNCVEREORNESISTIBIVILIORISTIS
VNISIQVAPLACETCVLTAPVELLASATEST
CVMTIBIPRAESERTIMPHOEBVSSVACARMINADO
NETAMONIAMQVELIBENSCALLIOPEALYRAM
VNICANECDESITIVCVNDISGRATIAVERBIS
OMNIAQVAEQVEVENVSQVAEQVEMINERVAP
ROBATHISTVSEMPERERISNOSTRAGRATISSIMAVIT
AETAEDIADVMMISERAESTNITIBILVXVRIAE
QVIDMIHITTAMMVTTASLAVDANDOBASSEPVELLAS
MVTATVMDOMINACOGISABIREMEA
QVIDALENONPATERISVITAEQVODCVMQVESEQV
ETVRHOCMAGISASSVETODVCERESERVITIO
TVLICETANTIOPAEFORMAMNYCTEIDOSETV
SPARTANAEREFERASLAVDIBVSHERMIONAE
ETQVASCVMQVETVLITFORMOSICORPORISAET
ASCYNTHIANONILLASNOMENHABERESIN
ATNEDVMSITEVISTVERITCOLLATAFIGVRIS

We end these exercises with a large, carefully composed sheet. Text, arrangement, and color can be chosen freely.

Katjenka Krause S

QVOD

Andrea Schmitz S

CREDOINVNVMDEVM
ICHGLAVBIANDENINE
GOTT

PATREMOMNIPOTENTE
MFACTOREMCAELIETTE
RRAEVISIBILIVMOMNI
VMINVISIBILIVM
DENALLMACHTIGENVA
TERSCHOPFERDESHIM
MELSVNDDERERDEAL
LERSICHTBARINVNDV
NSICHTBARINDINGE

ETINVNVMDOMINVMIE
SVMCHRISTVMFILIVM
DEIVNIGENITVMETEX.P
ATRENATVMANTEOM
NIASAECVLADEVMDED
EOLVMENDELVMINIDEV
MVERVMDEDIOVERO
VNDANDENEINENHERR
NIESVSCHRISTVSGOTT
ISHNGEBORENERSOHN
ERISTAVSDEMVATERG
IBORENVORALLERZEI
TGOTTVONGOTTLICH
TVOMLICHEWAHRER
GOTTVOMWAHRENG
OTT

GINITVMNONFACTVM
CONSVBSTANTIALEMP
ATRI
GEZEVGINGCHTGISCH
AFFENEINESWESENSMII
DEMVATER

PERQVEMOMNIAFACTA
SVNTQVIPROPTERNOS
HOMINESETPROPTERN

OSTRAMSALVTEMDES
CENDITDICAELIS
DVRCHINISTALLESGES
CHAFFENFVER VNSME
NSCHENVNDVMVNSE
RISHEILSWILLENISTER
VOMHIMMELHERABG
ESTIEGEN

ETINCARNATVSESTDESP
IRITVSANCTOEXMARI
AVIRGINEETHOMOFAC
TVSEST
ERHATFLISCHANGEN
OMMENDVRCHDENH
ILIGENGISTERAVSMA
RIADERIVNGERAVN
DISTMENSCHGEWOR
DEN

CRVCIFIXVSETIAMPRO
NOBISSVBPONTIOPILA
OPASSVSETSEPVLTVSEST
GECREVZIGTWVRDER
SOGARFVERVNSVNTE
RPONTIVSPILATVSHAT
ERDENTODERLITTENVND
ISTBEGRABENWORDE
N

ETRESVRREXITTERTIADIESE
CVNDVMSCRIPTVRAS
ERISTAVFERSTANDENA
MDRITTENTAGEGEMA
ESSDERSCHRIFT

ETASCENDITINCAELVM
SEDETADDEXTERAMPA
TRIS
ERISTAVFGEFAHRENIND
ENHIMMELVNDSIEZEZ
VRECHTENDESVATERS

Kerstin Krumwiede S

NMENSCHENE

CONNTESEZE

der obere scheitelpunkt
ergibt sich, je nach W...
des geschnittenen

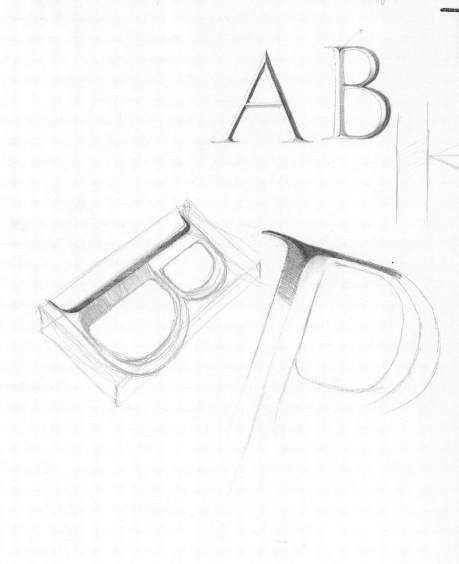

STEFAN RACHOW *S*

Negative Darstellung

We start preparations for the work on the monumental roman letters. Plaster casts introduce the first three-dimensional forms.

STEFAN RACHOW *S*

Positive Darstellung

Strichzeichnung der geschnittenen Mitte

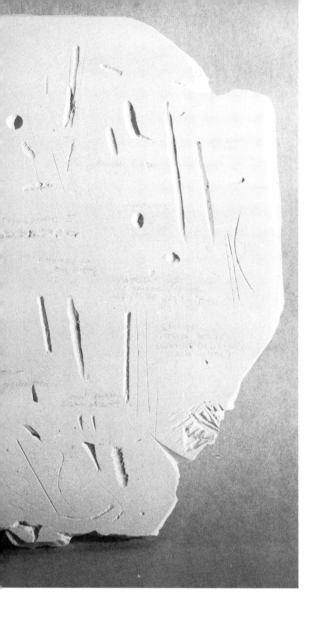

Monumental roman letters were used for inscriptions on buildings and epitaphs and on a multitude of other surfaces. They were chiseled into stone and magically come to life in the play of light and shadow. Practice slates of plaster or beeswax help students to explore the medium. We draw prototypes to discover relations between size and angles, and we use rubbings from originals. Knives and scrapers have to be used with utmost care. Plaster is a very brittle material, and it reveals the most minute mistakes.

Jan von Hugo S

NN

Beeswax mold

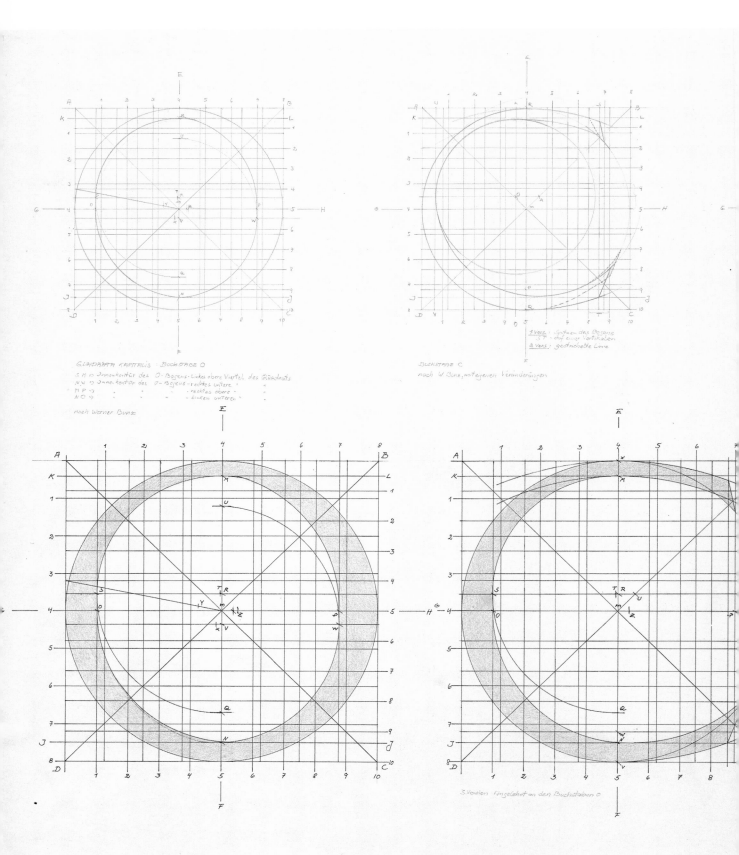

GUADRATA KAPITALIS : BUCHSTABE O

S M n Innenkontür des O-Bogens · Linkes obere Viertel des Quadrats
N W n Innen.kontür des O-Bogens · rechtes untere   "
M P n   "   "   "   "   - rechtes obere   "
N O n   "   "   "   "   - linken unteren   "

nach Werner Bunz

BUCHSTABE C

nach W. Bunz, mit geringen Veränderungen

1.vers.: Spitzen des Bogens
S.T. · auf einer Vertikalen
2.vers.: gestrichelte Linie

3.Version Angelehnt an den Buchstaben O

KARIN PEINERT S

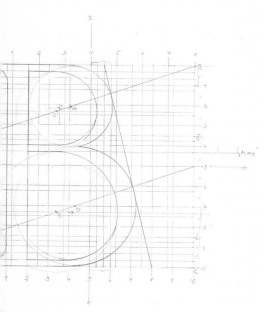

STADE B
W. Bume – mit eigenen Veränderungen

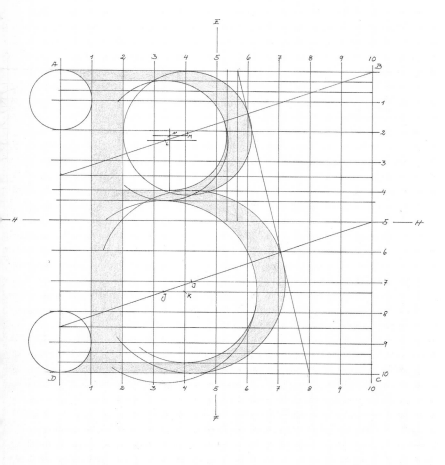

Karin Peinert S

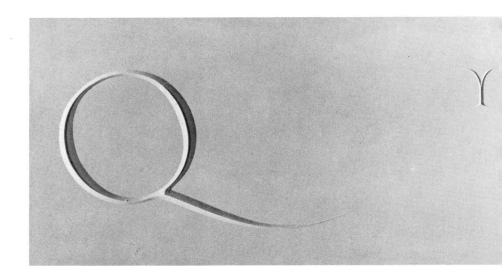

Knut Krahl S

Gertraud Baudy S

Gertraud Baudy S

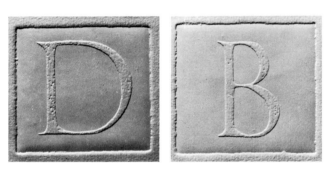

Blind stamping

NN

Blind stamping

Gertraud Baudy S

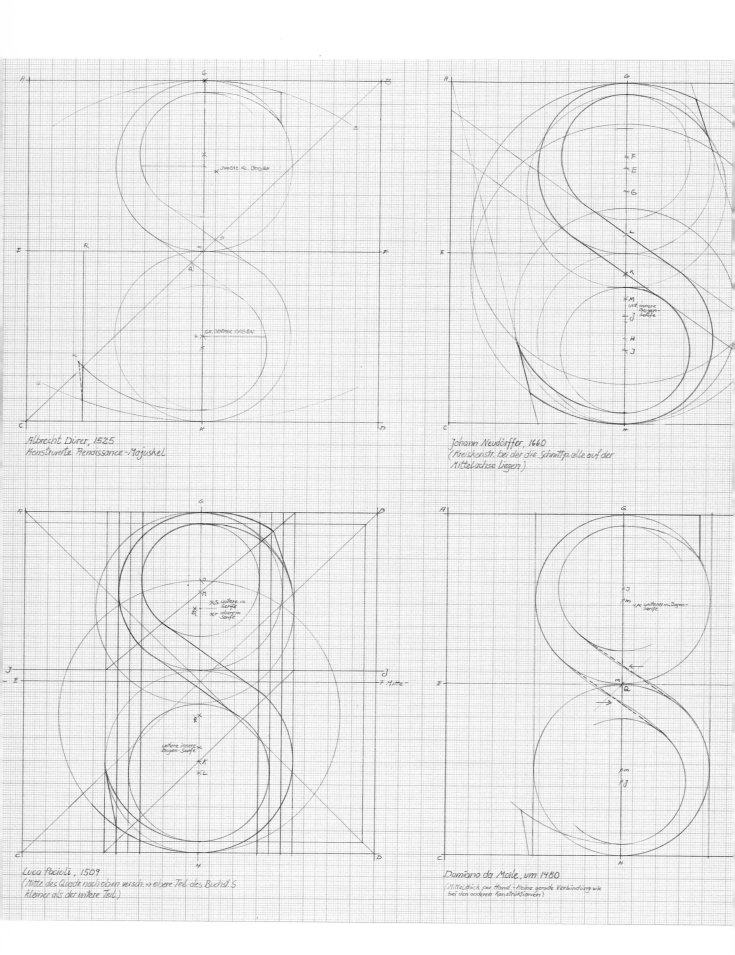

Albrecht Dürer, 1525
Konstruierte Renaissance-Majuskel

Johann Neudörffer, 1660
(Kreiskonstr. bei der die Schnittp. alle auf der
Mittelachse liegen.)

Luca Pacioli, 1509
(Mitte des Quadr. nach oben versch. → obere Teil des Buchst. S
kleiner als der untere Teil.)

Damiano da Moile, um 1480
(Mittelstück per Hand - kleine gerade Verbindung wie
bei den anderen Konstruktionen)

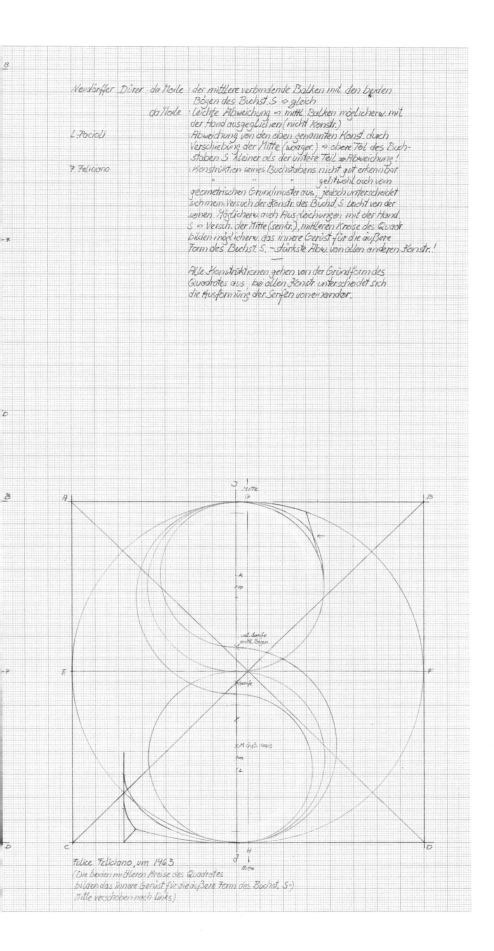

Neudörffer, Dürer, da Moile : der mittlere verbindende Balken mit den beiden
　　　　　　　　　　　　Bögen des Buchst. S ⇒ gleich
　　da Moile : leichte Abweichung ⇒ mittl. Balken möglicherw. mit
　　　　　　　der Hand ausgeglichen (nicht konstr.)
L. Pacioli　　　　Abweichung von den oben genannten Konst. durch
　　　　　　　Verschiebung der Mitte (wager.) ⇒ obere Teil des Buch-
　　　　　　　staben S kleiner als der untere Teil ⇒ Abweichung!
F. Feliciano　：Konstruktion seines Buchstabens nicht gut erkennbar
　　　　　　"　　　　"　　　"　　　geht wohl auch vom
　　　　　　geometrischen Grundmuster aus, jedoch unterscheidet
　　　　　　sich mein Versuch der Konstr. des Buchst. S leicht von der
　　　　　　seinen. Möglicherw. auch Ausgleichungen mit der Hand.
　　　　　　S ⇒ Versch. der Mitte (senkr.), mittleren Kreise des Quadr.
　　　　　　bilden möglicherw. das innere Gerüst für die äußere
　　　　　　Form des Buchst. S. ⇒ stärkste Abw. von allen anderen Konstr.!

　　　　　　Alle Konstruktionen gehen von der Grundform des
　　　　　　Quadrates aus, bei allen Konstr. unterscheidet sich
　　　　　　die Ausformung der Serifen voneinander.

Felice Feliciano, um 1463
(Die beiden mittleren Kreise des Quadrates
bilden das innere Gerüst für die äußere Form des Buchst. S.)
Mitte verschoben nach links)

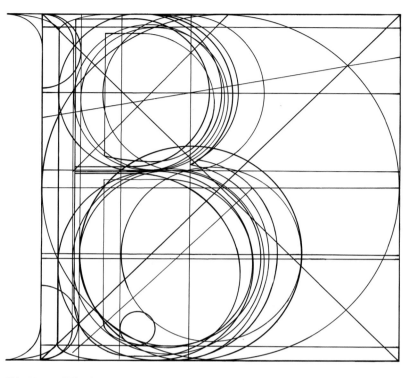

Felice Feliciano um 1463
Damiano da Moile um 1480
Wolfgang Fugger 1553

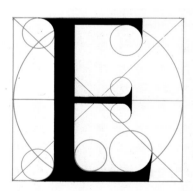

Luca Pacioli

Albrecht Dürer

Konstruierte Renaissance-Majuskel

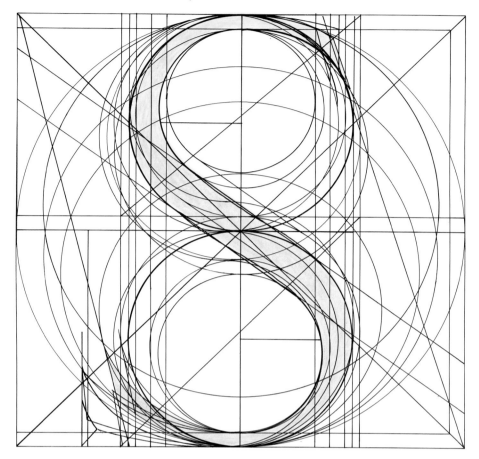

1. Johann Neudörffer, 1660
2. Albrecht Dürer, 1525
3. Luca Pacioli, 1509
4. Damiano da Moile, um 1480
5. Felice Feliciano, um 1463

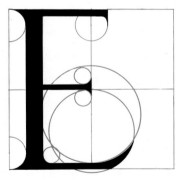

Johann Neudörffer

The works of different artists are enlarged to identical heights and superimposed upon each other with the help of tracing paper, so that the variations become very clear. The students are required to compose explanatory essays on the progress of their work.

KARIN PEINERT S

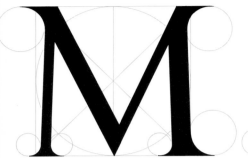

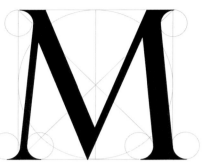

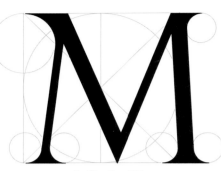

Luca Pacioli 1509

Albrecht Dürer 1525

Geoffroy Tory 1529

Konstruktion einer Renaissance Majuskel mit den drei geometrischen Grundformen. Entworfen 1509 von Luca Pacioli, (1455-1514) italienischer Franziskaner und Professor der Mathematik. Die vier Balken des Buchstabens bewegen sich innerhalb des Quadrats. Die Eckkapitälchen laufen teilweise stark aus dem Quadrat heraus. Das Breitenverhältnis zwischen den Balken beträgt 2:1. Ebenso das Verhältnis der Kreise zueinander. Der untere Punkt der zusammenlaufenden Mittelbalken ist gleichzeitig der Berührungspunkt der vertikalen Mittelachse mit der Basis des Quadrats.

Maler, Graphiker, Kunstschriftsteller, (1471-1528) Die Konstruktion basiert auf den theoretischen Erkenntnissen über die Formgesetze der Kunst, in Verbindung mit Gestaltungsmerkmalen nach optischen Gesichtspunkten. Das Balkenverhältnis beträgt 3:1. Die für die unteren Rundungen verwendeten Kreise haben alle den gleichen Durchmesser. Die untere Spitze ist leicht nach links aus der Mitte versetzt.

Auffallend ist die große Rundung im linken, oberen Bereich des Buchstabens. Ebenso das starke Heraustreten des rechten Balkens aus dem vorgegebenen Konstruktionsquadrat. Hieraus ergibt sich eine starke rechtsseitige Versetzung der mittleren Spitze des Quadrats. Das Kreisverhältnis, sowie das Verhältnis der Balken zueinander, beträgt 2:1. Der Buchstabe kippt leicht nach rechts.

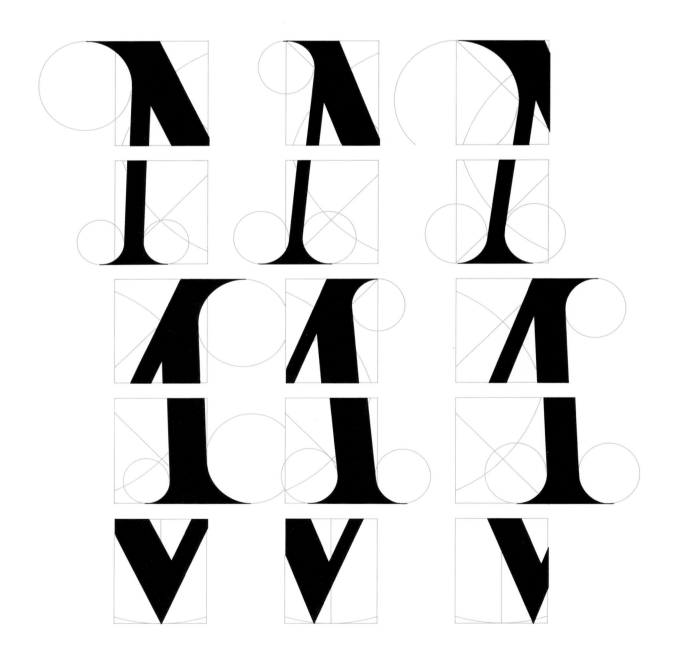

This phase is also con-
cluded with a final three-
dimensional piece. Details
have to be considered in
different planes. The text
provides clues to the shape
of the letters.

JENS RADEMACHER S

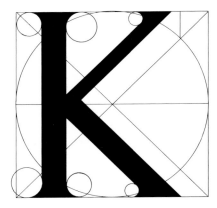

Luca Pacioli

Geburtsjahr: 1509

Größe Quadrat: 10 x 10 cm

Verwendete Kreisgrößen: 100 mm; 16 mm; 13 mm; 7 mm

Breite Senkrechte: 13 mm

Breite Aufstrich: 12 mm

Breite Abstrich: 7 mm

Besonderheiten: Beim Aufstrich sowie beim Abstrich an der jeweils rechten Kante kein Kapitäl vorhanden.

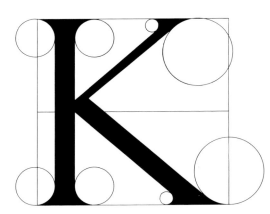

Johann Neudörffer

Geburtsjahr: 1660

Größe Quadrat: 10 x 10 cm

Verwendete Kreisgrößen: 36 mm; 20 mm; 6,6 mm

Breite Senkrechte: 10 mm

Breite Aufstrich: 10 mm

Breite Abstrich: 4 mm

Besonderheiten: Relativ kleine Kapitäle auf der jeweils rechten Kante beim Auf- sowie beim Abstrich.

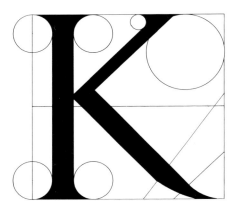

Albrecht Dürer

Geburtsjahr: 1525

Größe Quadrat: 10 x 10 cm

Verwendete Kreisgrößen: 40 mm; 20 mm; 8 mm

Breite Senkrechte: 11 mm

Breite Aufstrich: 11 mm

Breite Abstrich: 6 mm

Besonderheiten: Bei der von Albrecht Dürer konstruierten Schrift sind beim Aufstrich keine Kapitäle vorhanden – vielmehr läuft die Serife durch Verwendung von Kreisen die auf der rechten Begrenzungslinie des Quadrates ihren Mittelpunkt haben, spitz aus.

The last part of this chapter deals with classicistic roman letters (the typefaces of the nineteenth century). We switch from pen to pencil and work with rulers and compasses.

RENATE RUTENBERG S

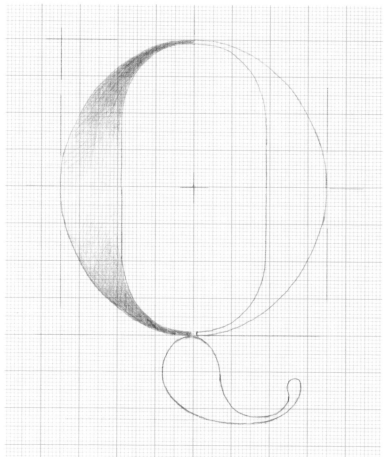

Renate Rutenberg S

nn

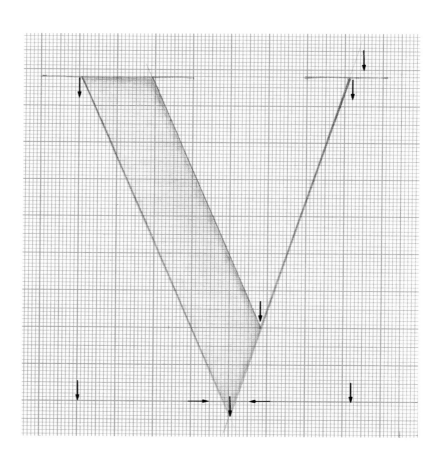

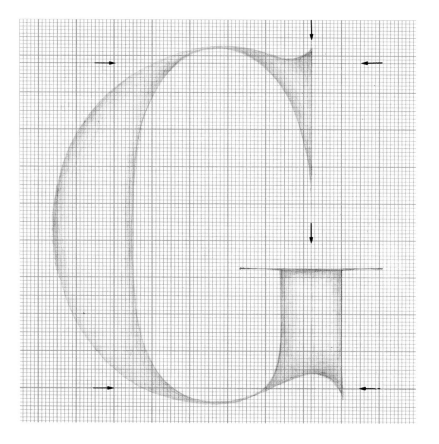

"Letters are the coinage of the mind — symbols."

NOVALIS

Renate Rutenberg S

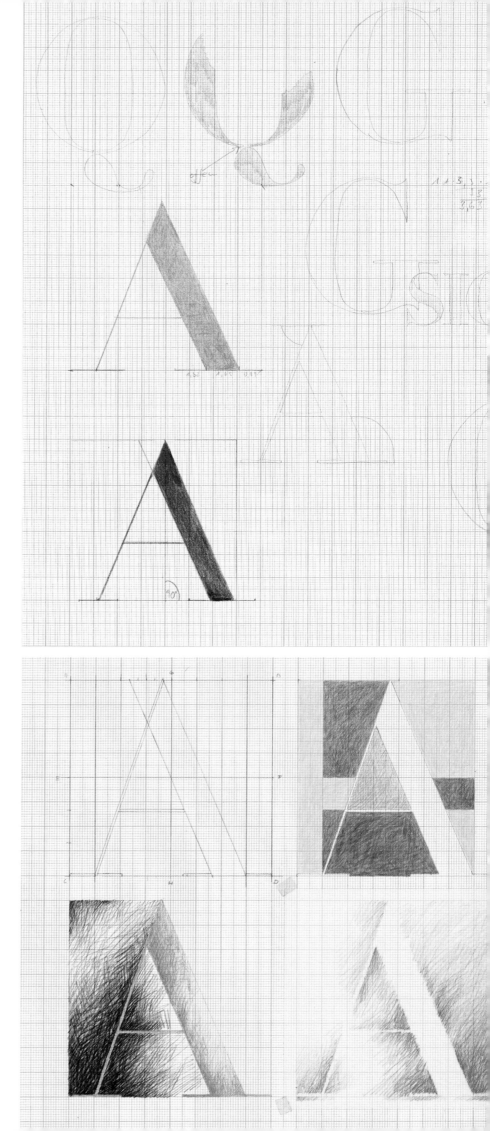

"As a traveler I felt obliged to visit the famous publisher Bodoni. I was pleasantly surprised. This Piedmontese is not at all conceited but practices his art with great passion. He showed me all his French prints and then he asked me whether I preferred the TELEMACHUS, the RACINE, or the BOILEAU. I had to confess that they seemed equally beautiful to me. 'Oh, but you are not looking at the title of the Boileau,' he replied. I examined it for quite some time, but I had to admit that I could not see anything out of the ordinary. 'Oh,' Mr. Bodoni exclaimed, 'BOILEAUDESPREAUX in one line of versal letters. It took me six months to find the right type!' "

STENDHAL

Our explorations start
with the writings of
Giambattista Bodoni,
Firmin Didot, or Justus
Erich Walbaum. Width
and height of the letters
and relationships of sizes
are carefully considered,
and measurements are
taken. The students are
introduced to typographi-
cal systems and design
their first metal type.

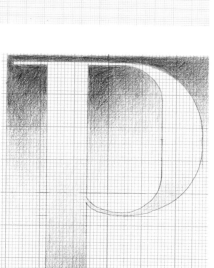

KARIN PEINERT S

KARIN PEINERT S

IV

In Gardens of Grace

THE VARIATIONS

My teachings continue with examples of the further development of writing within western culture. The students have to become aware of the magnitude of the creative influence that the Roman alphabet had on its successors. As before, history and practical exercises alternate.

There is much to chose from: Carolingian minuscule, fraktur scripts such as textura, Gothic script, rotunda, and civilité, art-nouveau-style scripts, sans-serif constructions, and three-dimensional works. Students are often eager to learn fractured scripts like textura, fraktur, and civilité, and even demand instruction in their use. The preceding training has enabled them to learn and understand new forms quickly.

Art nouveau holds a special fascination for many students. This style has always encouraged artists to use different craft techniques and gave a fresh impetus to practitioners of old skills. Works were executed in glass, enamel, wood, and linoleum. Etchings, weavings, and batiks were created. All these media were used for writing.

A note: Theoretical work has been done on most of the teaching units that I describe. I wish to draw attention to Falk Waldmann's publication, "Das Problem der gestalterischen Einheit von Schrift und Bild in der Buchtypographie: Eine gestalttheoretische Untersuchung am Beispiel relevanter englischer und deutscher Jugendstil-Buchgestalter" ("The Unity of Text and Illustration in Book Typography: An exploration of the works of influential English and German art-nouveau book artists"), (Hamburg, 1980, 2 vols.). Another example is Renate Fuhrmann's book, "Der Buchstabe Y: Herkunft und symbolische Bedeutung, Kontruktionen" ("The letter Y: Origins, symbolic significance, and constructions"), (Hamburg, 1983).

"Calligraphy is a creative art, the most thought-out form of writing. This art gives us the energy and inspiration to look ahead to a renewal of the art of typesetting."

EJNAR PHILIP

155

The consistent exposure to the graceful historical forms and to their diversity enriches the basis from which students can later draw inspiration for their own work.

"Making letters — in whatever form — is my greatest and purest joy. In different stages of my life it is to me what a song is to the singer, the painting to the painter, the joyful shout to the happy, and a sigh to the oppressed. It is to me the most complete expression of my life."

RUDOLF KOCH

esgibtdortvielekastaniensiestehenuberdemufer

undgehenauchinbischenindiestadthineinaufdiesen

sandwegenbirdorthinwosichdiewegezueinerstrasse

zusammentunwievielehändedenkstduverweisst

chonmitwievielhändenmandenwindaufhältauch

etztwoermüdeistimaugustmithundertdenkst

duuchwillfortgehenweilichimmernochnichtwei

wasdasistfortgehenaberichlerneesnichtderhimm

elistirgendwoundirgendwiehochundirgendwiebr

ttundtiefunddasmeerziehtsichzurücküberbahnen

vonschluckderwaldtrittüberdenflussbinaushin

hinaufdocherredetnichtumdasmoorliegendies

chlangendieunordnunggehtumhereswirddun

kelabermiegehtmanvonsichselberlfortwennid

dortgewesenbinunddortundimmernurwoichje

tztbinbeimirichweisjanichtwasichhierbinindie

verstadteinerderumhergehteinpaartagelangd

erniederfortfährtundetwasmitnimmtdieeru

e e f g h i k l m n n o p q r r r
r r t u x g f f h i k l m n n

h h b c d d e e e f g l m o p q r r
r f f r r t u x v v q x y z v v v

p q r r t m n z z z z g i u v r f f

NN

NN

möglichkeiten der wiederkehr
dem was war und woraufgegan
gen ist für ein paar schritte anhol
en - anholen jetzt gleich jetzt gle
ich weiß ß weiß ja nicht was ich
bin in dieser stadt
wer weiß schon mit wieviel händ
manden wind aufhält f hält
ich will ll fortgehen weil ich imm
noch nicht weiß was das ist fort
hn hinaber ich lerne es nicht der h
mel ist irgendwo und irgendwie
ch und irgendwie breit und tief
das meer zieht sich zurück über
en ausschließ der wald tritt übe
fluß hinauf doch er redet nicht
das moor liegen die schlangen
unordnung geht umher es wir
nee aber wie geht man von sich
er fort wenn ich dort gewesen bin
dort und immer nur woich jetzt

Noneri inprudens tatuumte Inquidame faciemtuum
Modoergo tufacquur quis talises· quadtabiminatur facero
dns· olloto atergetuo ·ubito uidero¡
dum haec idendem rimabundus examie delator
tua sum sund ait Byrrhena cuncta orae uides· Erum dictae
ceteros omnes remone secreto dacedere praecipit ortubus dispulsij·
omibus· Per hanc inouit deam o Luci carissime ut anxie tibi
metuo et ut pote pignori meo longe provisum cupio cave
tibi sed cave fortiter a malis artibus &2 facinoris illecebris
Pamphiles illius ortae cum· Milone isto orem dicis hospitem
nupta est magna primi nominis &2 lapillis &2 id genus
frivolis ihalatus omnem istam lucem mundi sideralis imis
Tarari &2 in vetustam caos submergere movit nam simul
oriemore conspexerit speciosae formae invenem venustate
euis sumitur &2 ilico ineum &2 oculum animam

At ego curiosus aliorum ut primum aras
magicae semper optatum nomen audivi
tantum a caudela Pamphiles
afiuit etiam ultro gestirem tali
magisterio me volens ampla cummercede
tradere &2 prorsus in ipso barathum

rota Alba maxima

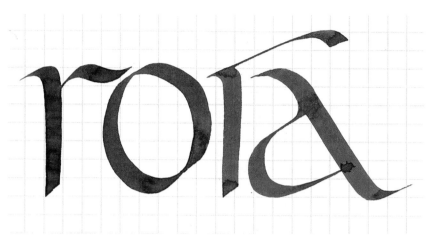

jeder papalagi hat einen beruf
es ist schwer zu sagen was dies ist
es ist etwas wozu man viel lust haben sollte
aber zumeist wenig lust hat
einen beruf haben das ist
immer ein und dasselbe tun

BODO KAEMMLE S

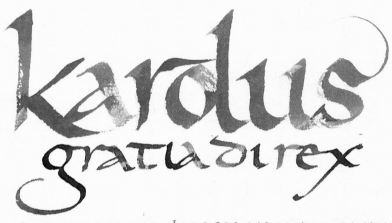

karolus gratia dei rex

CAPITVLA IVNIORIS KAROLI REGIS IN PISTIS EACTA

Notuesseuolumus omnib di & nris fidelibus qm haec quae secuntur er captcula nunc in istoplacitonro · Anno abincarnatione dni nri ihuxpi decc Lxiiii · Anno uidelicet regni nri ipso pro pitao xxv Inditionexij vii kL iul in hoc loco quidicitur piftisuna cusi deliunroru consensu Atq · consilio constituimus & cunctis sineulla refragatione perregnu nrm ob seruanda madamus ·

Primo considerauimus dehonore ecclesiaru & sacerdotu ac seruoudi & In muni tatereru ecclesiascicaru ut nullussibi deipsirebuscona aucto rttate presumat · & comtces epis et ministris ecclae Ineorummini teris adiutoresinom ndb · fiante sicut incaptulari predeces soru acpro genitoru nroru conti netur Insecundo libro cap xxiii erquicuq · comitu uelministroru reipub lice hitce quae mandamus obseruarenegle xertt · siprima & secundainco dehisad monitus non secorrexerit · ⬚

mea me confortat
promissio
mea me deportat
negatio

tempus est iocundum
o virgines
modo congaudete
vos iuvenes

tempore brumali
vir patiens
animo vernali
lasciviens

oh oh oh
totus floreo
iam amore virginale
totus ardeo
novus novus amor
est quo pereo

mea meum ludit
virginitas
mea me decludit
simplicitas

veni domicella
cum gaudio
veni veni pulchra
iam pereo

Armgart Gross *G*

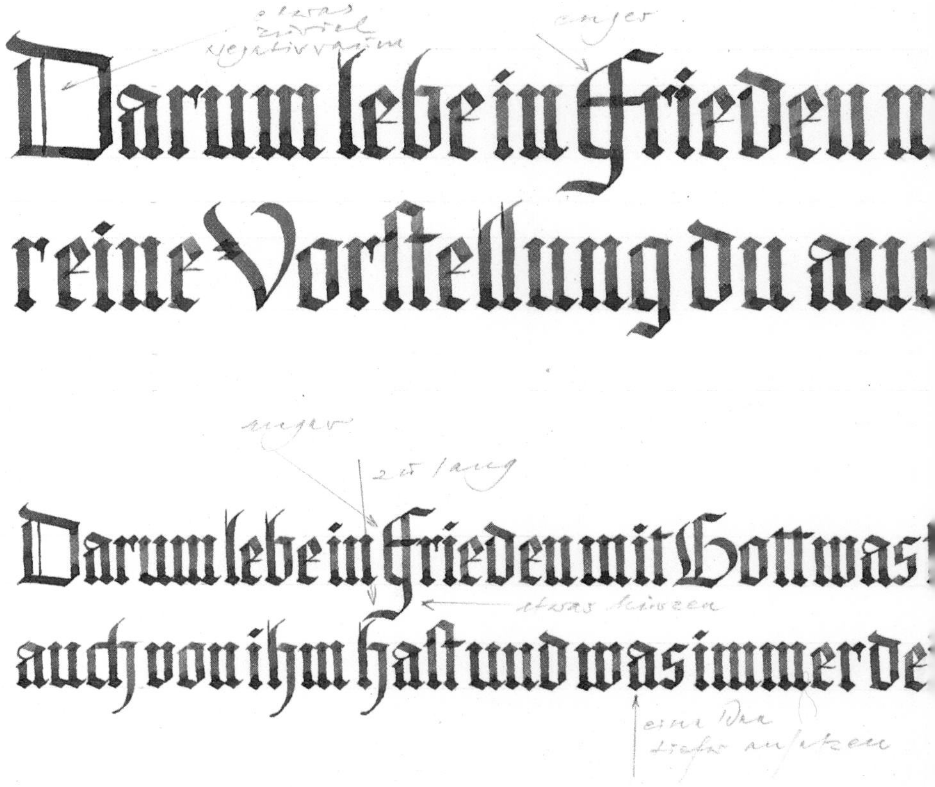

etwas zuviel Negativraum
enger
Darum lebe in Frieden m
reine Vorstellung du au
enger
zu lang
Darum lebe in Frieden mit Gott was
etwas breiter
auch von ihm hast und was immer de

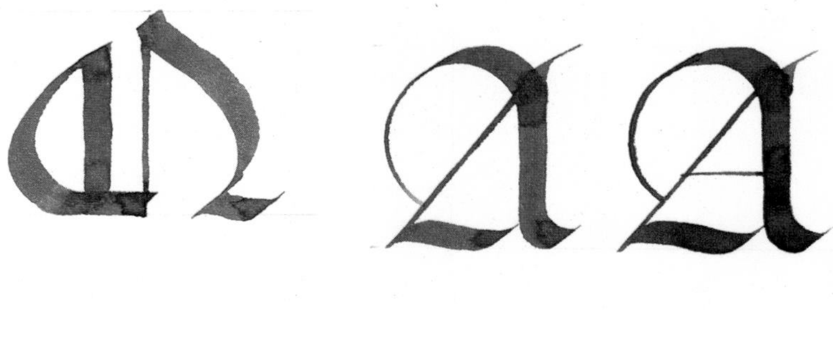

Gott was fie
on ihm halt

ne Vorstellung du
iehen und Sehuen

JENS RADEMACHER S

Günter Vortisch *A*

Aus dem hohlen Fin...
dringt ein buntes G...
Jeder sonnt sich heut...
Sie feiern die Aufe...
Denn sie sind selber auf...
aus niedriger Häus...
aus dem Druck von G...
aus der Straßen qu...
aus der Kirchen ehrw...
sind sie alle ans Lic...
Sieh nur, sieh! wie behe...
durch die Gärten u...
wie der Fluß, in Brei...
so manchen lustig...
und bis zum Sinke...
entfernt sich dieser...
Selbst von des Ber...
blinken uns farbig...
Ich höre schon des D...
hier ist des Volkes...
zufrieden jauchzet...
Hier bin ich Mensc...

So traenkt ein Sommertau die Erde,
Mir oft das Bild des Grabes braechte:
So lockt des Abends Dunkelheit
Zur tiefen Ruhe schoener Naechte.

Rüdiger Mohrdiek S

Andreas Gryphius /
Menschliches Elende /

Was sind wir menschen doch / ein wohnhaus grimmer schmertzen. / Ein baall des falschen gluecks / ein irrlicht dieser zeit. / Ein schawplatz herber angst / vnd wiederwertikeit / Ein bald verschmeltzter schnee vnd abgebrante kertzen. Dis leben fleucht davon wie ein geschwaetz vnd scherzen. Die vor vns abgelegt de s schwachen leibes kleid / Vnd in das todten buch der grossen sterblikeit / Laengst eingeschrieben sind / sind vns aus sinn vnd hertzen. Gleich wie ein eitell traum leicht aus der acht hinfaelt / Vnd wie ein strom v erscheust / den keine macht aufhaelt / So mus auch vnser nahm / lob ehr vnd ruhm verschwinden. Wa s itzund athem holt / faelt vnversehns dahin. Was nach vns kommen wird / wird vns ins grab nach zihn. Was sag ich. wir vergehn gleich als ein rauch von winden.

RENATE FUHRMANN S

Inclina Domine aurem tuam et exaudi me : quoniam inops et pauper sum ego. Custodi animam meam quoniam sanctus sum : salvum fac servum tuum Deus meus sperantem in te. Miserere mei Domine quoniam ad te clamavi tota die : laetifica animam servi tui quoniam ad te Domine animam meam levavi. Quoniam tu Domine suavis et mitis : et multae misericordiae omnibus invocantibus te. Auribus percipe Domine orationem meam : et intende voci deprecationis meae. In die tribulationis meae clamavi ad te : quia exaudisti me. Non est similis tui in diis Domine : et non est secundum opera tua. Omnes gentes quascumque fecisti venient et adorabunt coram te Domine : et glorificabunt nomen tuum. Quoniam magnus es tu et faciens mirabilia : tu es Deus solus. Deduc me Domine in via tua et ingrediar in veritate tua : laetetur cor meum ut timeat nomen tuum. Confitebor tibi Domine Deus meus in toto corde meo : et glorificabo nomen tuum in aeternum. Quia misericordia tua magna est super me : et eruisti animam meam ex inferno inferiori. Deus iniqui insurrexerunt super me et synagoga potentium quaesierunt animam meam : et non proposuerunt te in conspectu suo. Et tu Domine Deus miserator et misericors patiens et multae misericordiae et verax. Respice in me et miserere mei : da imperium tuum puero tuo et salvum fac filium ancillae tuae. Fac mecum signum in bonum ut videant qui oderunt me et confundantur : quoniam tu Domine adiuvisti me et consolatus es me.

Oremus : Aures tuae pietatis mitissime Deus inclina precibus nostris et gratia sancti Spiritus illumina cor nostrum : ut tuis mysteriis digne ministrare tibique aeterna charitate diligere mereamur. Deus cui omne cor patet et omnis voluntas loquitur et quem nullum latet secretum purifica per infusionem sancti Spiritus cogitationes cordis nostri ut te perfecte diligere et digne laudare mereamur. Ure igne sancti Spiritus renes nostros et cor nostrum Domine : ut tibi casto corpore serviamus et mundo corde placeamus. Mentes nostras quaesumus Domine Paraclitus qui a te procedit illuminet : et inducat in omnem sicut tuus promisit filius veritatem.

Quam dilecta tabernacula tua Domine virtutum : concupiscit et deficit anima mea in atria Domini. Cor meum et caro mea exsultaverunt in Deum vivum. Etenim passer invenit sibi domum : et turtur nidum sibi ubi ponat pullos suos. Altaria tua Domine virtutum rex meus et Deus meus. Beati qui habitant in domo tua Domine : in saecula saeculorum laudabunt te. Beatus vir cuius est auxilium abs te : ascensiones in corde suo disposuit in valle lacrimarum in loco quem posuit. Etenim benedictionem dabit legislator ibunt de virtute in virtutem : videbitur Deus deorum in Sion. Domine Deus virtutum exaudi orationem meam : auribus percipe Deus Jacob. Protector noster aspice Deus : et respice in faciem Christi tui. Quia melior est dies una in atriis tuis super millia. Elegi abiectus esse in domo Dei mei : magis quam habitare in tabernaculis peccatorum. Quia misericordiam et veritatem diligit Deus : gratiam et gloriam dabit Dominus. Non privabit eos qui ambulant in innocentia Domine virtutum : beatus homo qui sperat in te.

De profundis clamavi ad te Domine : Domine exaudi vocem meam. Fiant aures tuae intendentes in vocem deprecationis meae. Si iniquitates observaveris Domine : Domine quis sustinebit. Quia apud te propitiatio est : et propter legem tuam sustinui te Domine. Sustinuit anima mea in verbo eius : speravit anima mea in Domino. A custodia matutina usque ad noctem speret Israel in Domino. Quia apud Dominum misericordia : et copiosa apud eum redemptio. Et ipse redimet...

Pgraphica articalli I

Magnus

Carolus Pius Felix Augustus.

Die gotifche Schrift war urfpruen
lich eine reine Kleinbuchftabenfchrift
Deshalb heißt die fruehe Form auch

Die gotifche Schrift war urfpruenglich eine reine Kleinbuch-
ftabenfchrift · Deshalb heißt die fuehe Fruehe auch gotifch
Minuskel · Die gotifche Schrift und die daraus entwickel
Deshalb heißt die fruehe Form

q q q q q p

r r r r r

abcdefg

y z

JENS RADEMACHER S

Stadtmaus und Feldmaus · Eine Stadtmaus ging spazieren und kam zu einer Feldmaus, die tat ihr guetlich mit Eicheln, Gersten, Nuessen und womit sie konnte. Aber die Stadtmaus sprach Du bist eine arme Maus. Was willst du hier in Armut leben. Kome

Romme mit mir, ich will dir und mir genug schaffen von allerlei koestlicher Speise. Die Feldmaus zog mit ihr hin in ein herrlich schoenes Haus darin die Stadtmaus wohnte und gingen in die Kamner da war vollauf von Brot Fleisch Spec Wuersten Kaese und allem Da sprach die Stadtmaus Nun iß und sei guter Dinge solcher Speise habe ich taeglich im Vberfluß Indes kam der Kellermeister und rumpelte mit den großen Schluesseln an der Tuer Die Maeuse erschraken und liefen davon Die Stadtmaus fand bald ihr Loch Aber die Fel

dmaus wußte nirgendhin liefen davon lief die Wand auf und ab und hatte ihr Leben aufgegeben Da der Kellner wieder hinaus war sprach die Stadtmaus Es hat nun keiner Not laß uns guter Dinge sein Die Feldmaus antwortete Du hast gut sagen Du wußtest den Loch fein zu treffen dieweil bin ich schier vor Angst gestorben Ich will sagen was die Meinung ist Bleibe du eine reiche Stadtmaus und friß Wuerste und Speck ich will ein armes kleines Feldmausle in bleiben und meine Eicheln essen Du bist keinen Augenblick sicher vor dem Kellner vor den Katzen vor so viel Mausefallen und ist dir das ganze Haus feind Solches alles bin ich frei und sicher in meinem armen F

eldloechlein In großen Wassern saengt man große Fische aber in kleinen Wassern faengt man gute Fischelein Wer reich ist hat viel Neider Sorge Gefahr · Vom Raben und Fuchse ein Rabe hatte einen Kaese gestohlen und setzte sich auf einen hohen Baum und wollte zehren Als er aber einer Art folgend nicht schweigen kann wenn er isset hoerte ihn ein Fuchs ueber den Kaese kecken und lief zu ihm und sprach O Rabe nun hab ich mein Lebtag keinen schoeneren Vogel gesehen von Federn und Gestalt denn du bist Vnd wenn di auch so eine schoene Stimme haettest zu singen so solt man dich zum Koenig kroenen uber alle Voegel Den Raben kitzelte

solch Lob und Schmeicheln fing an vollt sein schoenen Gesang hoeren lassen Vnd als er die en Schnabel auftat entfiel ihm der Kaese Den nahm der Fuchs behende fraß den Kaese und lachte des toerichten Raben Huet dich wenn der Fuchs den Raben lobt Huet dich vor Schmeichlern die schinden und schaben Huet dich vor boesen Nachbarn oder schicke in Geduld willst du mit bese Leuten wohnen. Denn es goennet niemand dem andern was Gutes · Diese beiden Fabeln schrieb Martin Lu

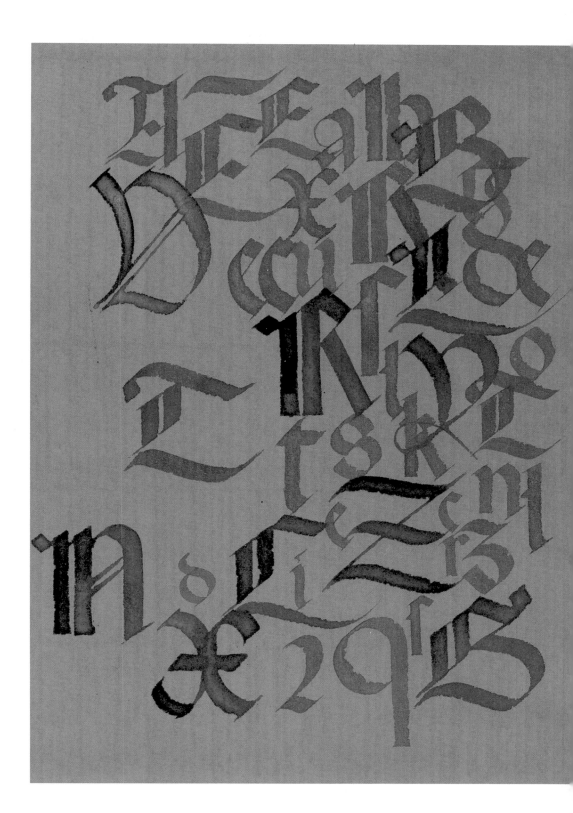

Ihis rebus pace confirmata post di
quartum quam est in Britannian
ventum naves de quibus supra d
emonstratum est quae equites su
stulerant ex superiore portu leni
vento solverunt/ ⁋ quae cum adpr
opinquarent Britanniae et ex cast
ris viderentur/ tanta tempestas sub
ito coorta est/ ut nulla earum cur
sum tenere posset/ sed aliae eo den
unde erant profecte/ referentur·
aliae ad inferiorem partem insula
e quae est propius solis occasum m
agno suo cum periculo deicerent
ur/ quae tamen ancoris iactis cu
m fluctibus complerentur nesse
sario ⁋ adversa nocte in altum pri

Ihis rebus pace confirmata post di
quartum quam est in Britannian
ventum naves de quibus supra d
emonstratum est quae equites su
stulerant ex superiore portu leni
vento solverunt/ ⁋ quae cum adpr
opinquarent Britanniae et ex cast
ris viderentur/ tanta tempestas sub
ito coorta est/ ut nulla earum cur
sum tenere posset/ sed aliae eo den
unde erant profecte/ referentur·
aliae ad inferiorem partem insula
e quae est propius solis occasum m
agno suo cum periculo deicerent
ur/ quae tamen ancoris iactis cu
m fluctibus complerentur nesse
sario ⁋ adversa nocte in altum pri

Non ha che far niente con la fame,
che fa do vero, pur ella ci arrivi. ~
Passon gli amanti star senza le dam
i mesi e gli anni, e mantener vivi
Ma se due di del consueto stam
i poveracci mai rimagno privi,
e basta: che de fatto andra gli ved
a porre il capo dove il nonno ha pie

Desta l'aurora omai dal letto scappa
e cava fuor le pezze di bucato:
Poi batte il fuoco, e cuocer fa la pappa
pel suo giorno bambin che allora e nat
e febo ch'e il compar, gia con la cappa
e con un bel vestito di broccato ~
che a nolo egli ha pigliato da breg
tutto splendente viensene al corte

Das Wort frei bedeutet hier ohne Zweckbindung aber nicht unbedingt zwecklos · Meist handelt es sich um Texte aus der Literatur oder dem

JENS RADEMACHER S

Talche si vien da questi effetti in chiaro
che d' more la fame e piu potente
onde che ognun di lui piu qesta ha caro
e quando a la sue ore ei non la sente
lamentasi, e il pare ostico e amaro
Percio riceve torto da la gente;
mentre ciascun la cerca e la desia
e s'ella viene, vuol mandarla via

efigli con licenza de superiori e privilegio

Ne per ancora le gnanesi genti
anno veduto comparire in scena la
materia che da il portante a' denti,
tende al corpo nutrimento e lena:
Percio molti ne stanno malcontenti
che son usi a tener la pancia piena;
e ben si scorge a una mesticia tale,
che la mastican tutti piu che male.

venezia mdcclxxviii presso antonio yata

HERMANN FRÜHLING A

176

SIGRID ENGELMANN *(Ikarus)*

Sed haec eloquendi praecepta sicut cogitationi sunt
necessaria ita non satis ad vim dicendi valent
nisi illis firma quadam facilitas quae apud
graecos nomitur accesserit ad quam scribendo
plus an legendo an dicendo conferatur solere
quari scio quod esset dilligentius nobis etiam
si qualiber earum rerum possemus una esse
contenti verum ita sunt inter se et indiscreta

Left: NN

wê war umbe volge ich tumbem wâne,
der mich sô sêre leitet in die nôt ?
	ch schiet von ir gar aller fröiden âne,
daz sie mir trôst noch helfe nie gebôt.
	 och wart ir varwe liljen wîz und rôsen rôt,
und saz vor mir diu liebe wolgetâne
	eblüejet rehte alsam ein voller mâne :
der ougen wunne und des herzen tôt.

	in stæter muot gelîchet niht dem winde :
ich bin noch alse sî mich hât verlân,
	il stæte her von einem kleinem kinde,
swie wê sî mir nû lange hât getân
	kswîgende ie genôte unde ein verholner wâ,
swie dicke ich mich der tôrheit underwinde,
	wâ ich vor ir stân,
und sprüche ein wunder vinde,
	ich muoz doch von ir ungesprochen gân.

Ich hân sô vil gesprochen und gesungen,
	âz ich bin müede und heis von mîner klag
ich bin umb niht wan umb den wind betw
	it sî mir niht geloubet, daz ich sage,
wie ich sî minne
	nde ich sô holdez herze ir trage.
dêswâr mirn ist nâch werde niht gelunge
	æte ich nâch gote ie halb sô vil gerunge
er næme mich hin zuo zim ê mîner tage.

Right:
Stefanie Siekkötter S

Oft anstaunt ich dich· stand an gestern begonnenem
fenster· stand und staunte dich an· noch war mir di[e]
neue stadt wie verwehrt· und die unüberredete lan[d]
schaft finsterte hin· als wäre ich nicht· nicht gaben
die nächsten dinge sich müh· mir verständlich zu
sein· an der laterne drängte die gasse herauf· ich
sah· das sie fremd war· drüben das zimmer· mitt[eil]
bar· geklärt in der lampe· schon nahm ich teil· sie
empfanden es· schlossen die läden· stand· und dann
weinte ein kind· ich wußte die mütter rings in
den häusern· was sie vermögen· und wußte alle[s]
weinens zugleich die untröstlichen gründe·
oder es sang eine stimme und reichte ein stück
weit aus der erwartung heraus· oder es hust[ete]
unten voller vorwurf ein alter· als ob sein
körper im recht sei wider die mildere welt·
dann schlug eine stunde· aber ich zählte zu
spät· sie fiel mir vorüber· wie ein knabe· ei[n]
fremder· wenn man endlich ihn doch den ba[ll]
nicht fängt und keines der spiele kann· die
die andern so leicht an einander betreiben

abcdefg
hijklm
nop

qrsſt
uvw
yꝫ

GÜNTER VORTISCH *A*

"... this ingenious art, to paint words, to speak with one's eyes and to reveal thoughts to the heart with nothing more than different lines and vague shapes."

GUILLAUME DE BRÉBEUF

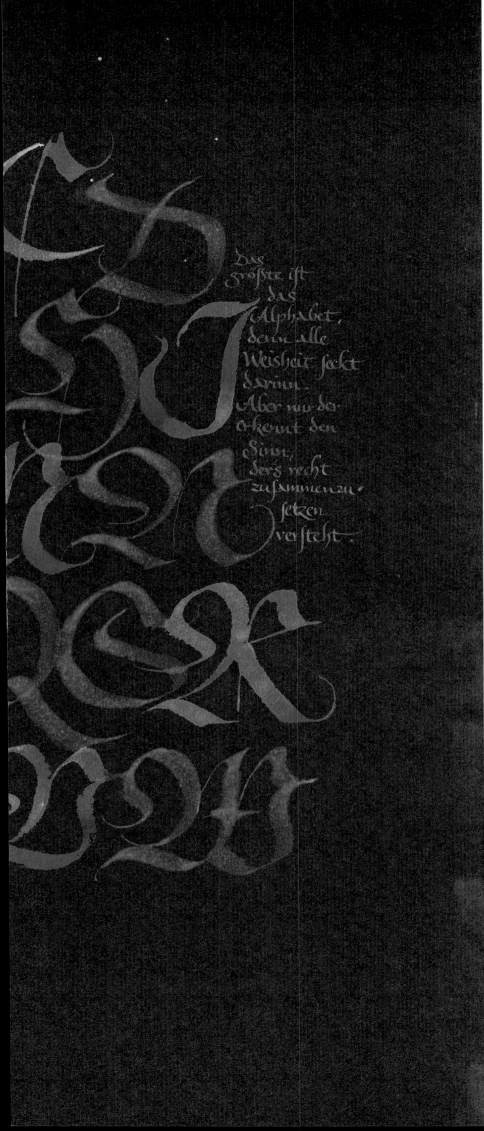

Das
größte ist
das
Alphabet,
denn alle
Weisheit steckt
darinn.
Aber nur der
erkennt den
Sinn,
der's recht
zusammenzu-
setzen
versteht.

GÜNTER VORTISCH *1*

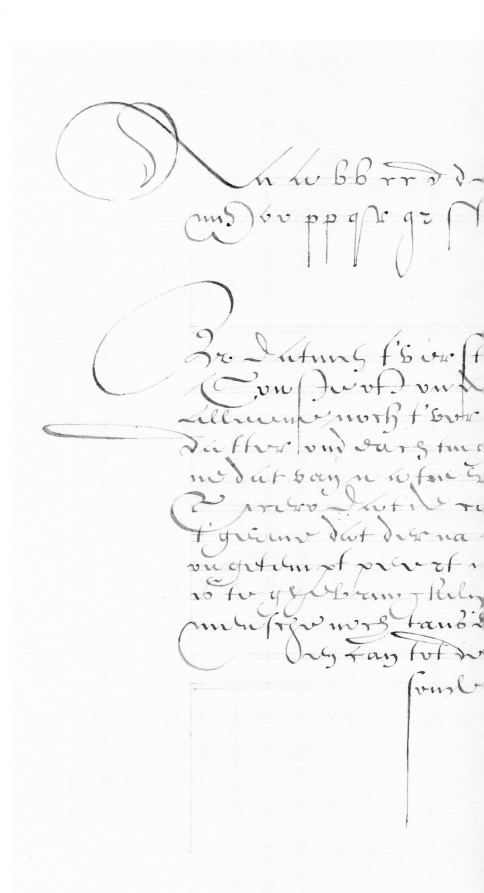

186

"Writing is the image of speech:
the more similarities the better."

VOLTAIRE

In 1895 Otto Eckmann designed a type for the Ruthardt foundry in Offenbach on the Main river. It carries his name, and we use it as the basis for our art-nouveau-style exercises. We use Japanese brushes, since the well-known flowing forms cannot be achieved with wide- or thin-nibbed pens. The letters are shaped by the oriental technique of lowering the brush onto the paper at a right angle.

TORIL MARØ HENRICHSEN S
(NORWAY)

EGTOVERSKOGO
MELUNDERDERM
EFAARJESOVAO
NKRANSAVLLLKON
VALLOGJEGHARING
ENALMANAKKOGIN
GENPENGERNEIJEG
HARNATURENSVAN
DRINGSSANSSOMV
ARSLERTIDOGSTED
VEIOGHAGOGNATT
OGVAAROGHOESTE
RVANDRINGSMENN
SOMJEGNAARKVEL
DENSTENGERFORM
INFOTDATARJEGH
ARTTENAVOGMOE
RKETFALLERIMITT
FALNGOGSKJULER
STIOGSTAVOGSOL
GAAROPPOGSOLG
AARNEDVEDVOGGE
OGVEDGRAVMENFO
ERJEGSLUTTERVIS
ENAVVILJEGENJOR
DENSSOENNFAATA
KKEFORDETAAPNES

Originalsize

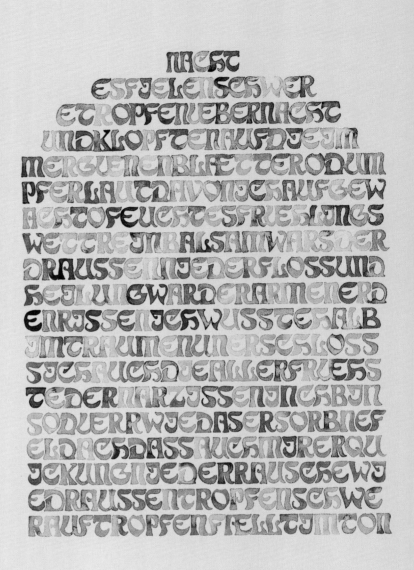

DIELEIBER·WELCHENICHTSGEFUN
DEN·ENTTAEUSCHTUNDTRAURIGVO
NEINANDERLASSEN·UNDWENNDIEM
ENSCHEN·DIEEINANDERHASSEN·IN
EINEMBETTZUSAMMENSCHLAFEN
MUESSEN·DANNGEHTDIEEINSAMKEIT
MITDENFLUESSEN·

Magdalene Hanke-Basfeld *S*

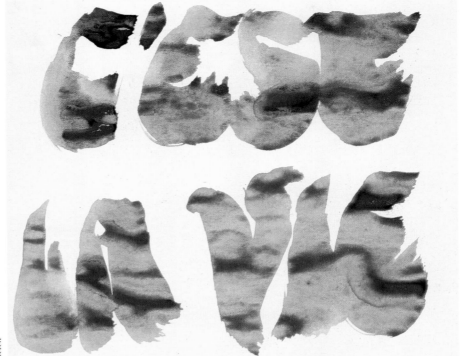

Marlies Kendzia S

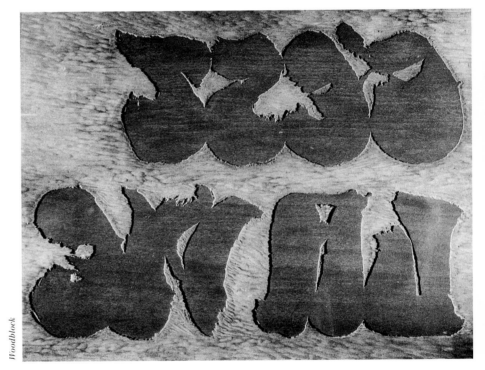

Woodblock

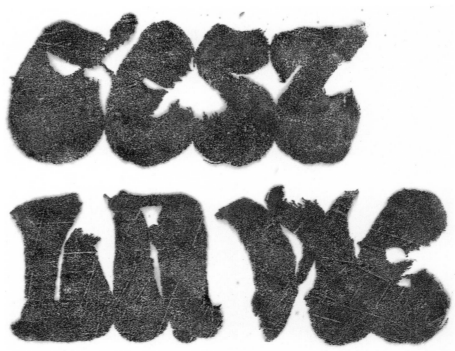

Print

FALK WALDMANN S

Woodcut

KATHARINA HENRICI S

Needlework

Reverse painting on glass

MARTINA OTTO S

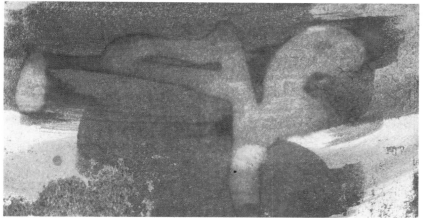

Bodo Kaemmle S

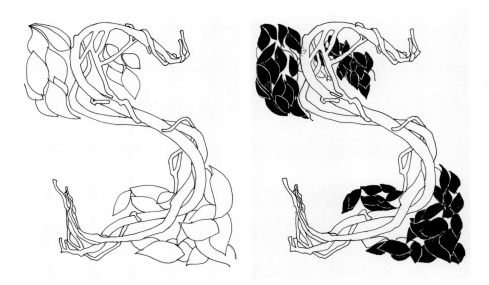

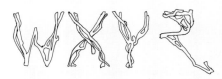

Erfindung eines Alphabets,
angeregt durch den Haaaleu
Teil des Titelbildes in dem
Jahrbuch NOVISSIMA von
Antonio Rizzi, Mailand 19.

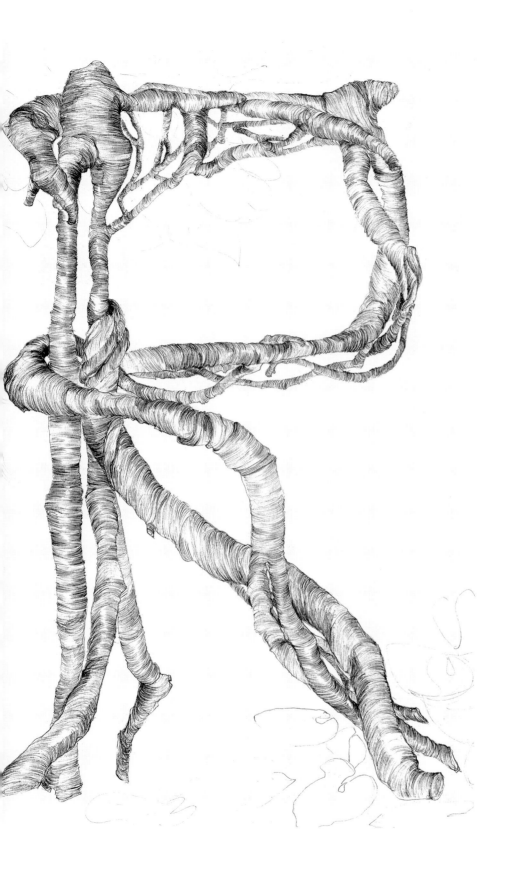

RENATE KNOTH-REGNIER S

LEFT:
HEINER ZWANCK *S*

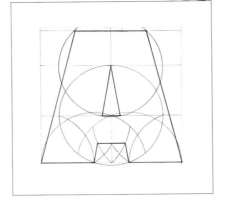

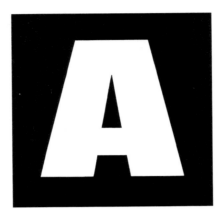

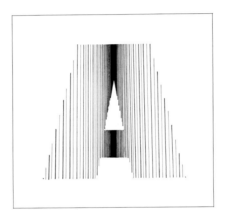

RIGHT:
REINHARD UND CHRISTINE DE ROOY *S*

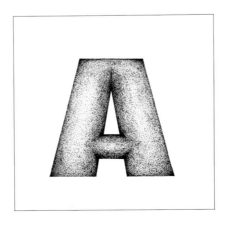

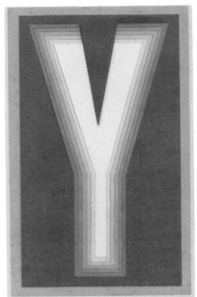

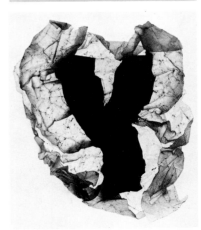

HEINER ZWANCK S

V

The Echo of Language

INTERPRETATIONS

*The Use of the Alphabet
to Visualize Linguistic Events*

Two thousand years of development in our western culture have yielded a rich supply of variable forms. The hand has learned to control them and make them visible.

The basis for a true understanding of a given text lies in recognizing and correctly interpreting historical forms of writing. This process requires hard work. Texts generate emotions that express themselves through the hand that guides the pen. This highly individualized sequence can transform letters to the point of illegibility. The result is a psychogram of the author or the writer.

The written interpretation of a text differs from a spoken version in only one point: it is visible instead of audible. Pathos, gestures, and presentation in both cases come from the same source: the mind, stimulated by emotion.

The writer interprets texts, uses the alphabet as a tool, but is free of lines, measures, and punctuation. He is, however, subjected to his own repertoire of form, and he alone bears the responsibility for the artistic and aesthetic quality of the finished work.

Concentration, silence, and composure are prerequisites for a successful interpretation of a text into a written medium. Meditation, appropriate breathing techniques, and an understanding of body rhythms help create the desired state of mind.

Rüdiger Mohrdiek S

Was du tust ist aussicht

gut du hast es begriffen   gib es zu   aber finde dich nicht damit

mann mit dem stein   niemand dankt dir   kreidestriche

markieren   den tod   freu dich nicht zu früh   das aussicht

mit eigener tragik   duzen sich wechselbälge vogelscheuchen

sprich mit der sonne ein wort   während der stein rollt   aber lab dich an dei

sondern   vermehre um einen zentner   den zorn in der welt   um ein gram

stumm aufrauend wie gras   die hoffnung   ihr geläch

rollend   rollend ihren zorn auf die   berge

MICHAEL KNIPPRATH S

er regen lecke sie gelangweilt auf

ist   keine karriere

auguren

schweig

macht nicht

herrscht ein mangel an männern in der welt
das aussichtslose tuend

zukunft

hans magnus enzensberger

MICHAEL KNIPPRATH S

karl greift zum karl aber schon hat karl
? karl mit karl auf den karl
? mit karl auf den karl karl kommt
? da stosst karl auf karl und
? karl karl stosst auf ueber karl
? karl ueber karl aber karl gibt
? weiss war er will und karl brennt
? karl hat sich verbrannt und karl
? gibt nicht auf karl weiss war er
? reisst aber karl gibt nicht auf
? er will karl greift ueber karl
? und da steht karl karl ist da
? befaellt ein karl karl und karl be
? karl und karl ahnen dass karl
? karl gegriffen habe karl ge?
? entfaellt karl gefaellt sich und karl
? karl gibt nicht auf karl weiss
? ueberfaellt karl wie karl und
? der karl einfach vor karl und
? karl karl bohrt den karl in den
? karl den karl am karl zum karl
? karl mit seinem karl von karl auf
? den karl gekehrt und durch karl
? von karl entfernt blicken fragend
? erklaert karl karl da will karl
? packen doch karl verbirgt sich
? karl da deckt karl karl karl auf
? karl von konrad bayer 1961

michael knipprath 1985

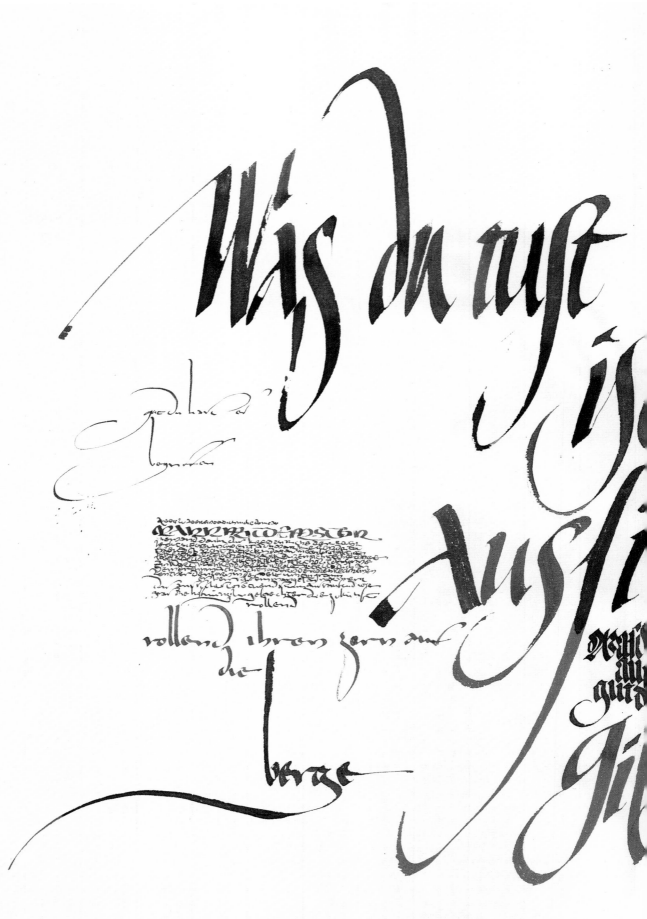

Mann mit dem Stein

hans magnus enzensberger

MICHAEL KNIPPRATH S

WERWENNICHSCHRIETHÖRTEMICH
DENNAUSDERENGELORDNUNGEN
UNDSELBSTESNÄHMEEINERMICH
PLOETZLICHANSHERZICHVERGINGE
VONSEINEMSTÄRKEREMDASEIN
DENNDASSCHÖNEISTNICHTSALS
DESSCHRECKLICHENANFANGDENWR
NOCHGRADEERTRAGENUNDWIR
BEWUNDERNESSOWEILESGELASSEN
VERSCHMÄHTUNSZUZERSTÖREN
EINJEDERENGELISTSCHRECKLICH
UNDSOVERHALTICHMICHDENN
UNDVERSCHLUCKEDENLOCKRUF
DUNKLENSCHLUCHZENSACHWEN
VERMÖGENWIRDENNZUBRAU
GENENGELNICHTMENSCHEN
NICHTUNDDIEFINDIGENTIERE
MERKENESSCHONDASWIR
NICHTSEHRVERLÄSSLICHZU
HAUSSINDINDERGEDEUTETEN
WELTESBLEIBTUNSVIELLEICHT
IRGENDEINBAUMANDEMABH
ANGDASSWIRTÄGLICHWIEDER
SAHENESBLEIBTUNSDIESTRA
SSEVONGESTERNUNDDASVER
ZOGENETREUSEINEINERGEW
OHNHEITDERESBEIUNSGEFIEL
UNDSOBLIEBSIEUNDGINGNICHT
RMR

ARMGART GROSS *G*

BODO KAEMMLE *(Ikarus)*

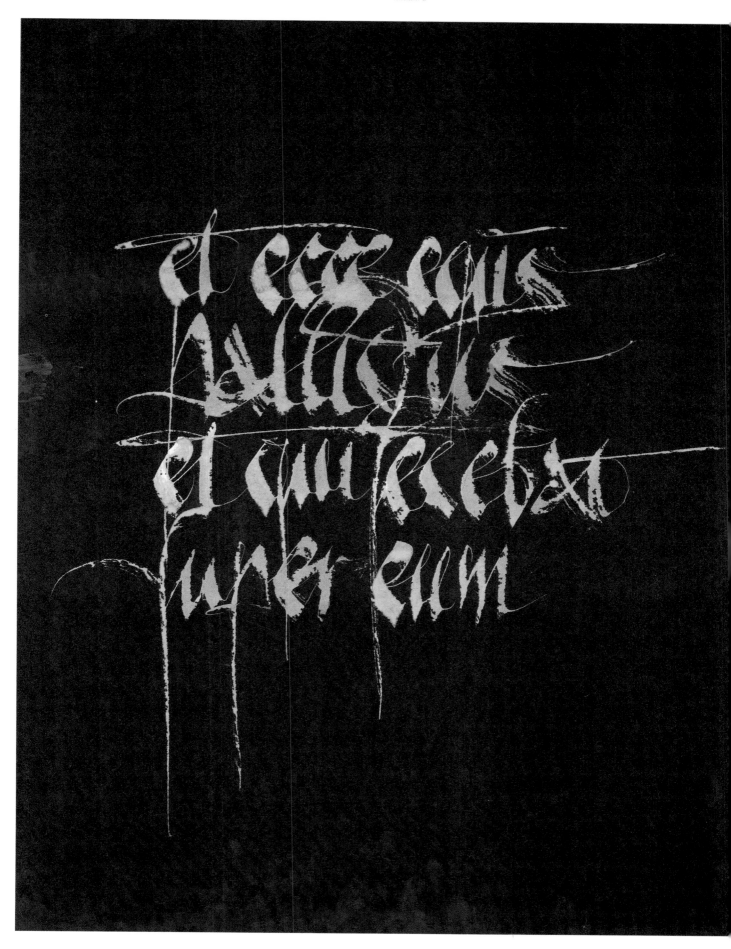

zochseciiz
nettrageaip
niehtparait
ichtnlycet
dienmiact
garje-rfeik
denkgiechei
chorulaiaget
docznarjen
mernialeich
coraiserrera
zoicangia
detrichiget
diereichate
ripaeredieni
runerzeurzii
nrodierdiene
rrnnrzneeia
aeichavernnt
lerennitrrera
zeraiterijred

deine zwogn find och forben

que guardan el camino y la ribera

no reza que los álamos cantores ... a un olivero seco

habitado de ... misteriosas ... el olivero hendido por el rayo

... en su mitad podrido

ejércitos de hormigas en hilera ... con las lluvias de abril y el sol de mayo

ya trepando por él y en sus entrañas ... algunas hojas verdes le han salido

... el olivero centenario en la colina

urden sus telas grises las arañas ... que lame el Duero, un musgo amarillento

aquí que describe oliveto ... Duero ... le mancha corteza blanquecina

con su hacha el leñador ... el carpintero ... el tronco carcomido y polvoriento

te convierta en ... sena de campana ... no reza cual los álamos cantores

brazo de canto o yugo de carreta ... que guardan el camino y la ribera

antes que rojo en el hogar mañana ... habitado de pardos ruiseñores

ardas de alguna miseria casera ... al borde de un camino

antes que te devore un torbellino ... y tronche de soplo de las sierras blancas

hasta que el río hacia el mar te empuje por valles y barrancos

olivero quiero anotar en mi cuaderno la gracia de tu rama verde

mi corazón espera también hacia la luz y hacia la vida otro

milagro de primavera

ANTONIO MACHADO

Ursula Gärtner *A*

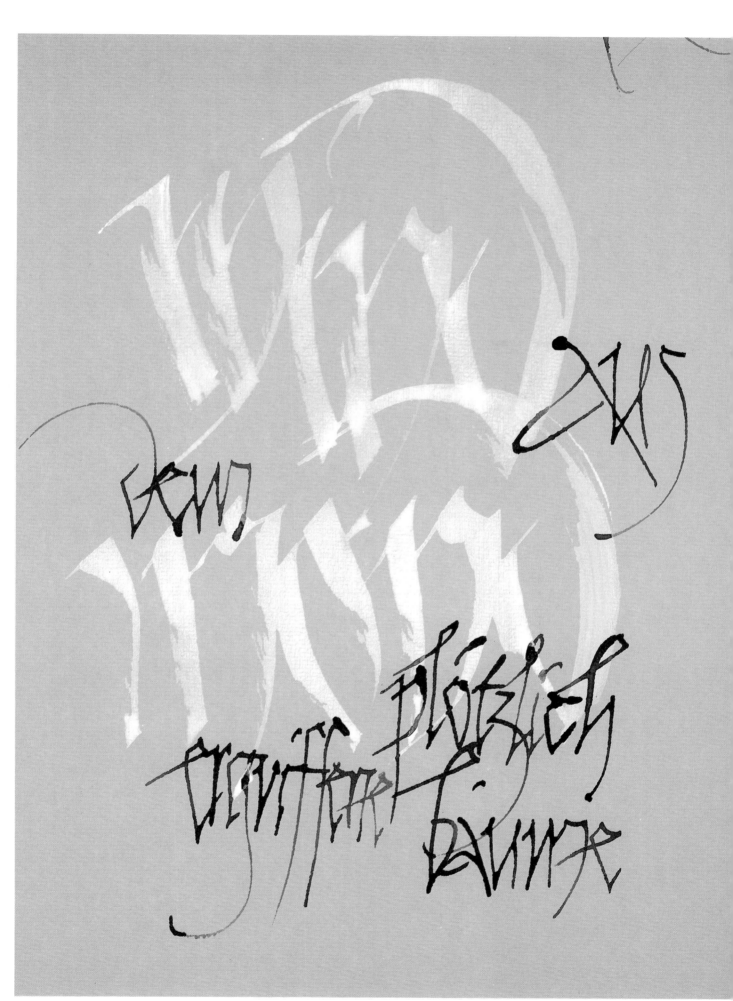

KARIN ISERLOTH *(Ikarus)*

I Vere dulci
 Mitten in dem
mediante,
 frühlingsheire,
non in Maio, paulo ante,
 Im April roth, wie ich meine,
Luce solis radiante;
 Stand im hellen sonnenscheine
virgo vultu elegante
 wohl der schönsten mädchen eine
fronde stabat sub vernante
 ynderm grünen laub alleine
canens
 flötend
cum cicuta.
 auf dem wege.

II Illuc veni fato dante
 Kam ihr dorten just entgegen.—
nympha
 jeder
non est
 nymphe
equipollens
 konnte ihr nichts
eius plante!
 ihr neid erregen!
que me viso festinante
 ängstlich floh sie meinetwegen
greges fugit cum balante,
 Ihre ymbfohr auf schmalen stegen
meto dissoluta.
 zierlich irs geheg.

III Clamans tendit
 Ich ihr nach
ad ovile
 quer durch die heide.—
hanc sequendor precor: »sile!«
 »hilfe!« rief sie— »halt, o maide,
nichil timeat hostile!«
 halt, ich zu dir nichts zuleide!«
precor spernitret monile,
 zeigte ihr ein klein geschmeide,
quod ostendi, tenet vile
 doch ymsonst, trotz meiner eide
virgo; sic locuta:
 war ihr myrd nichts träge:

Mitten in dem frühlingshaine

IV "Murur
"Kann
vertrum",
ist dein
inquit, "nolo,
geschenk verzichten,
quia plena estis dolo!"
wald nichts von bösewichten!"
comprehendam rei volo;
doch im gras sie zu bestrichten;
clarior
— etwas schönres,
non est sub polo
gibts mitnichten —
vilibus induta.
war ich rasch und rege

"quid fecisti",
"räuber!"
inquit,
fing sie an
"prave!
zu klagen,
ve ve tibi! tamen ave!
"wie wir kommest du dies wegen!
ne reveler, ulli cave,
aber wir nichts weitersagen,
ut vim domi tuta!
weil ich sorge hege.

V Satis illi fuit grave,
Urgern schien sies zu ertragen,
michi gratum
mir doch wars
← et suave.
ein wohlbehagen.

VI Si reverit meus pater
Vater und der bruder wachen
vel Martinus
strenge über
maior frater,
solche sachen,
erit michi dies ater;
hätte wahrlich nichts zu lachen;
vel si saret mea mater,
müsster würde gar zum drachen,
cum sit antue
mir die hölle
peior quater,
heiss zu machen,
virgir cum tributa!"
und es setzte schläge."

de kachelaben jeden freitagmorge
drop ick mi in en gaststuv an de kai
mit mien groten broder paul op'n
krügel beer broder paul is twee joh
oller as ick un wi snackt vun de
olen tieden gewestern is ook wedd
weisst noch paul sä ick un wi wir

negenteihnhunnertuntwee du harst
dien erste ries mookt as schippsjung rou
round the world op de elsflechter ba
hanna heye grod achter di nu wedder
anmunstert op de viermaster perotis
as lichtmatros ich wer to de tied no
schooljung un veerteihn johr un k

kaom an bord op besöök wat er oben
noch kien fierobend un du saust sei
di mol man so lang int logis ich kriom
denn woll bald ick kiek mi dat denn
schipp an de himmelhogen riggschaft
un de tweedusend tamp un slarpd
denn no de mannschaftslogis hin isk

waschlappens nu harr wi so woll all uns geschenk
opa dutt de jagd doarch tweeun twintig wihnac
htliche geschenkparadiese wuorn to unr blotroch
in de parfumerie orissen wi gau noch onr rinken
von wegen de letzten poor kleenigkeiten for denn
un for dat ontekolonie for tante alice lippenstift
fur tante ysabel noglack for ihre lavendelseep
rasierwasser for opa und all so lome adriane wate
onren fred is hart is feinopr zettel in de lust wou
ruch barg kundschaft un in de lust wuorn ruch bro
wohlgeruche unr parsien indien haiti honoluli

un sankt pauli op den tresen sturen un hericht
dekorative deughbore pyramiden in forern unr
un stilisierten darnnboom huengen obenher
zuckerkringel an sonnern luden waschlappen
ton utsoriken wol dess de nette verkaufrin un
de nekrung tosooriental nud a adriadne derg
waschlappenboom nuen poor waschlappens
wuille wi onr noch ontruhenen frauen sa
disse ont de onroschers un ont de bottenboom
yenne sae dat nette frauen oncht zusomoen
bechtehn oonrk funfzig bitteschoen wat sae ick

for onre waschlappens sossteinomrk un schu
präsident sae dat frouen handgewobt ertw
un professor schauonarken selfsopinrd hau
hoazy und ytschodosijard och so sae ick unt
track onen briefbuch wenn dat son supirwa
schuppens suund denn suund de se for den pry
so onlat geschenkt pakken se uns onn in o du
salye o du froachliche wohlstand du waschlap
pens nu harn wi so woll nu all uns geschenk
opa dutt de jagd doarch tweeun twintig wih
nachtliche geschenkparadiese kleenigkeiten for

PETER TOKARSKI *A*

JENS RADEMACHER S

RENATE FUHRMANN S

Rüdiger Mohrdiek S

GESA DENECKE .S

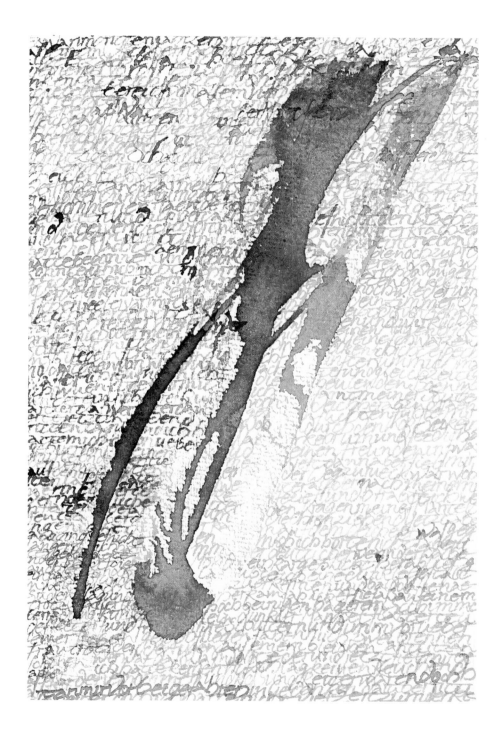

Jutta Nachtwey S

RENATE SUBEL S

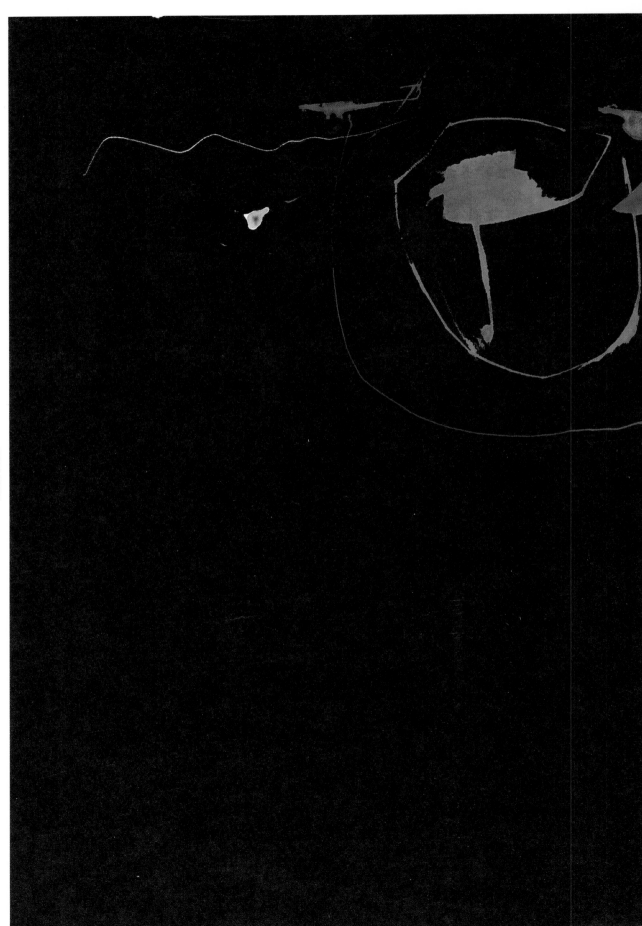

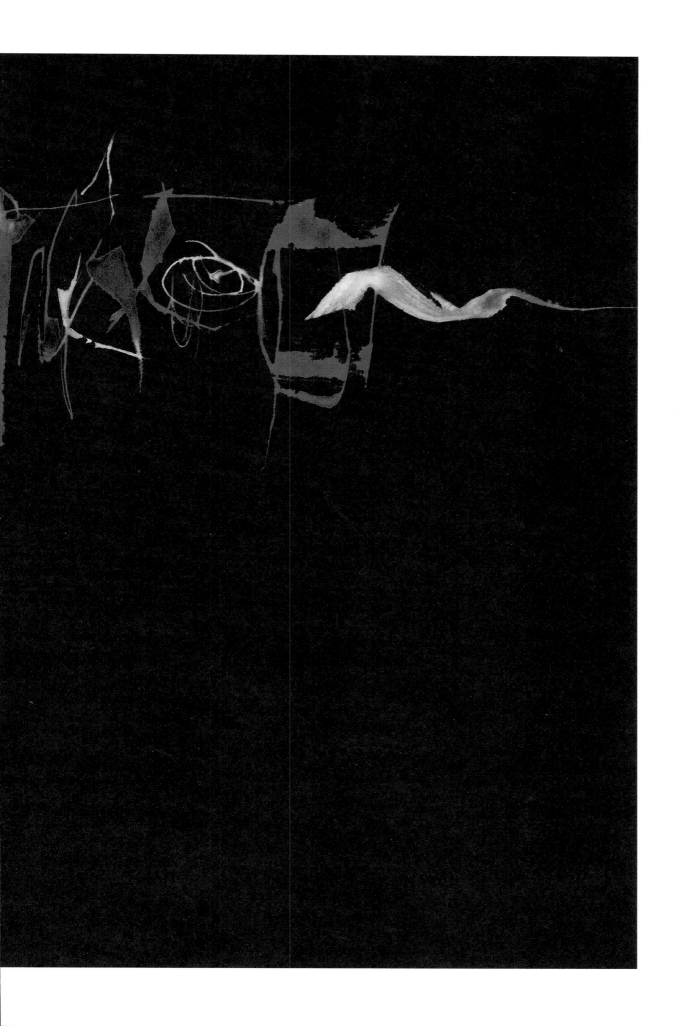

Over the course of years I have observed students and their intellectual and manual skills very carefully. The insights that I have gained are represented in the teaching methods that are described and illustrated in this book.

The core of my educational efforts is the ever-changing balance of guided exercises and joyfully free activity. With a solid foundation of seeing, knowing, and doing, the student will be well equipped to venture into new realms of writing. Many of the requirements are all but forgotten, but skill and dexterity are obtainable goals for the student who submits to the demands of a serious education in writing.

The prerequisites are devotion, passion, and composure.

GLOSSARY

ALPHABET

A collection of signs that represent all sounds of a particular language.

BASTARD SCRIPT

A form of writing that uses elements from two or more sources.

BLOCK LETTERS

Old name for sans-serif roman letters. The basic strokes are of equal weight.

CALLIGRAPHY

The art of beautiful writing.

CIPHERS

Symbols and numbers.

CIVILITÉ

A French fractured script of the sixteenth century.

CODEX

A series of parchments that came into use after rolls of text. From the fifth century on, a particular arrangement of information—the predecessor of today's book.

COLOPHON

An inscription usually placed on the last page of a handwritten book. It may contain information about the writer or about the production of the work itself.

CURSIVE

Writing in which the letters are joined together.

DUCTUS

The strokes that make up letters.

EGYPTIAN

A sans-serif roman letter with lines of identical width, but with exaggerated horizontal strokes.

EPIGRAPHY

The study of inscriptions.

EVANGELS

Handwritten copy of the Gospels.

EX LIBRIS

A phrase, meaning "from the library of," used on book plates before the owner's name.

FIGURE ALPHABETS

Human or animal bodies shaped into letters to decorate precious manuscripts. Their history is extensive.

FRAKTUR

A style of letter whose predecessor was Gothic script, round Gothic, and Schwabacher scripts. They were fractured roman scripts. Fraktur is a more complicated version of the above-mentioned forms. There was no specific German script, as some historians and calligraphers imply. These writing forms were popular all over Europe.

FROTTAGE (RUBBING)

A rubbing can be taken from any surface with a negative or positive relief. Best results are obtained by using a pouch made of porous fabric and filled with graphite dust in place of a pencil.

GOTHIC SCRIPT

Various fraktur scripts, developed vertically with a gridlike character. In use during the thirteenth to fifteenth centuries.

GOTHIC MINUSCULE

The Carolingian minuscules of the thirteenth century were changed by fracturing the round forms. The result was the Gothic minuscule; its most influential version was missal script.

HALF UNCIAL

Further development of the uncial, dating from the fifth to the ninth century. The beginnings of lowercase writing.

HANDMADE PAPER

Paper made from raw materials such as linen, hemp, or silk and ladled from a vat onto a screen.

INITIAL

A large, sometimes elaborately decorated first letter of a text.

ITALIC

Upper- and lowercase letters with a slant to the right, very rarely to the left.

JAPANESE PAPER

A fibrous paper made by hand from plant pulp. It is very elastic and is especially suited to lettering that is executed with a brush.

LIGATURE

A connection between two or more letters.

MAJUSCULE

A large or uppercase letter.

MARGINALIA

Explanatory notes written in the margins of a text.

MINUSCULE

A small or lowercase letter.

MISSAL

A book that contains text and notes of the spoken and sung parts of the Roman Catholic liturgy.

MONOGRAM

A formation consisting of several single letters.

PALEOGRAPHY

The study of handwritten documents.

PALIMPSEST

A sheet that has been written on more than once, after the first text has been removed. This occurred only on parchment.

PSALTER

A collection of the psalms of the Old Testament.

RAG PAPER

Paper made from textile remnants.

ROMAN CAPITALS

Uppercase roman letters that were in use throughout antiquity.

ROTUNDA

A version of Gothic script developed in fourteenth-century Italy. The angular forms of the letters appear more rounded.

RUNES

A form of writing used by Germanic tribes. It can be traced back to before Christ and to earlier roots in Alpine areas. It is very rarely used in books.

SCHWABACHER

A rough, fraktur script of the early fifteenth century. The origin of the name is unknown.

GLOSSARY

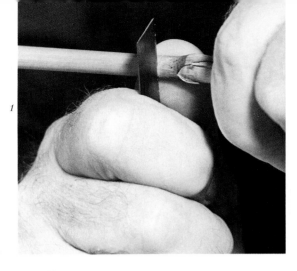

SCRIPT (WRITING)

Without tools writing is impossible. In
Europe the most widely used pen has a
wide nib and leaves a thin or thick line
depending on the direction of the stroke. It
used to be made from common natural
objects like reeds and quills from geese,
pelicans, swans, or ravens. Today it is more
likely made of steel.

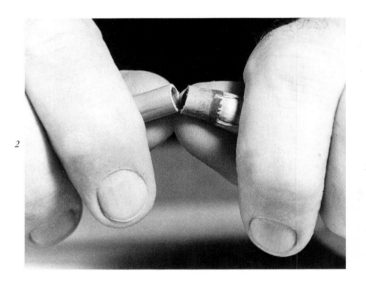

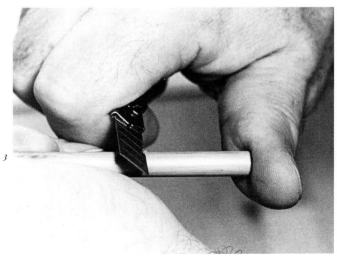

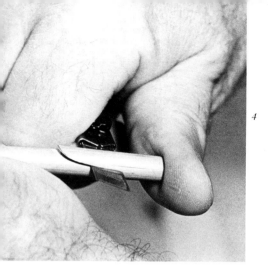

4   *How to make a pen*
The following illustrations explain the function of a reed pen. Reeds should be harvested between November and March and cut as close to the ground as possible. After a drying period of several weeks, they are cut into pieces about 10 inches long. Since the shafts taper towards the tip, the width of the pens can be regulated easily.

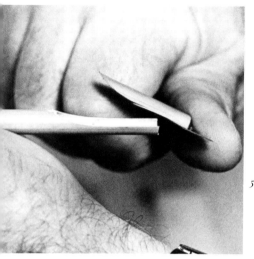

1

Cut at a right angle about 1/2 inch behind the node.

2

Break the pieces apart.

5   *3   4   5*

Place a blade 2 inches from the break and cut the reed in half lengthwise.

6

6

Scrape out the pulp with the fragment that was just cut.

7

7

The second cutting step. Make the second cut about 1 inch from the tip. This produces a flat and wide end that can be sharpened on both sides to achieve a crisp edge.

GLOSSARY

8

9

8   9

To guarantee a constant flow of ink, the
pen needs to be split horizontally. To avoid
an excessively long split, drill a hole with a
heated needle at the point where the second
cut was made.

10   11

The cut between the hole and the tip is best
done on a small wooden block of cross-cut
timber.

10

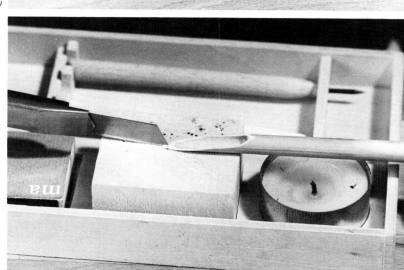

11

12

13

12
The final touch is a slanted cut across the tip, which determines the width of the nib.

13
The finished pen.

The life span of a reed pen is short. With intensive use it may wear out in days, or it may last for some weeks. Quills are more durable. Prepare them the same way. Both produce a flexible stroke, and they are the models for all industrially produced metal pens.

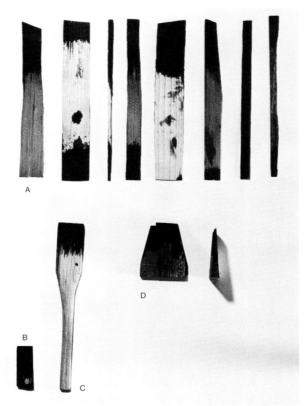

Handmade writing tools
A Strips of wood veneer
B Simple wood chips
C Simple wood spatula
D Veneer on a base of cherry wood
(hardwood)

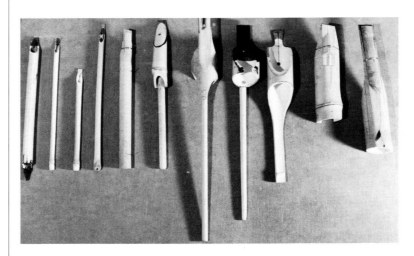

Bamboo pens. Bamboo is a very hard
material and requires tools like bench vises
and saws. The largest one of the pictured
pens is 15 inches long with a width of
almost 1 inch. All the pens were made by
Michael Knipprath and Günter Vortisch.

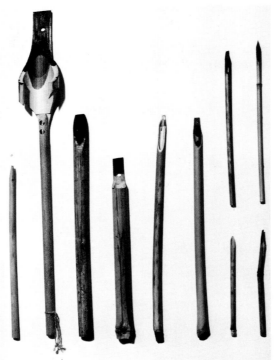

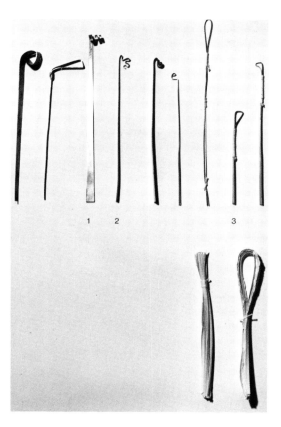

Writing tools fashioned from zinc wire.
Zinc is very soft and can easily be shaped
with pliers. The ends are secured by manila
ties. These tools are not pens by any
definition. The ink is trapped in the loops,
which determine the resulting line. 1, 2,
and 3 are examples.
Similar implements can be made from
paper.

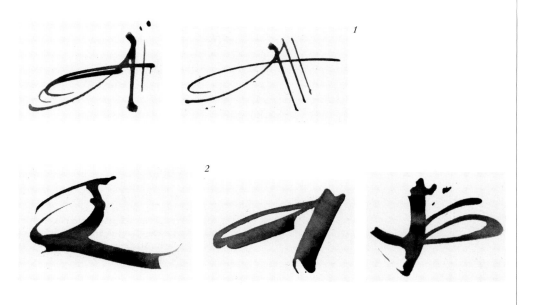

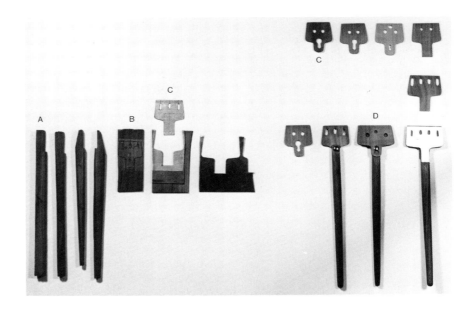

These pens are small works of art. The pen holders are made of rosewood; the nibs and reservoirs are brass and can be exchanged.

A Raw form for pen holders

B Nib pattern

C Ink reservoir

D Finished pen

They were designed and made by the architect Herman Frühling, and we are currently testing them.

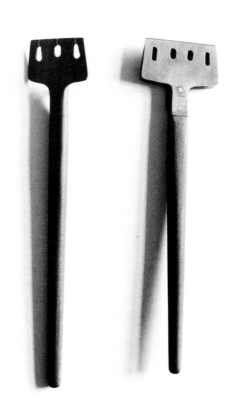

Stroke patterns

Almost no pressure should be applied. The movement of the pen modulates the stroke and is dependent on the type of writing and the writer's experience. The examples show italic.

1   2

Light upstroke and full downstroke.

3

A tilt onto the right corner of the pen for a fine upstroke.

4   5   6

Downstroke for a descender arching to the left (half pen used).

2

3

1

4

5

6

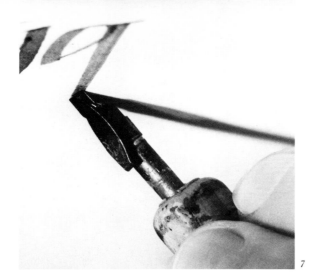

7

Lightly tapered full downstroke formed by a slight twist of the pen.

8

Crossed "g." Started with the full width of the pen. At the end of the stroke it is tilted to the right corner.

9

Crossed "e."

10

"L" loop.

11

"R" downstroke, started from full width.

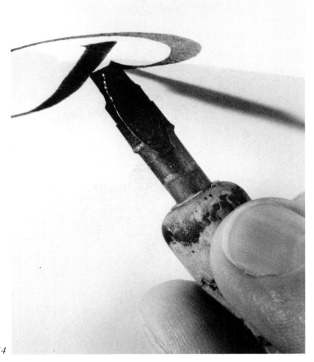

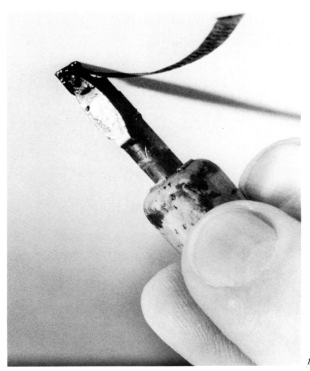

12

Thin and wide stroke of a full pen.

13

Full up- and downstroke and connection to the fine end line of the "G" curve, drawn from right to left.

14

Endstroke of a capital "P," half pen slightly lifted.

15

Downstroke and left swing of a descender. The pen is slightly pushed to the left.

16

"X" downstroke, slight thickening at the end; the pen is slightly pushed upwards.

GLOSSARY

STENOGRAPHY

A shorthand, interestingly the only script in use today that discerns between fine and wide strokes.

TACHYGRAPHY

A shorthand consisting of a system of syllables.

TIRONIC NOTES

A roman shorthand named after the inventor Tullius Tiro, one of Cicero's freed slaves who copied his master's speeches in the senate.

TYPOGRAPHY

The art of typesetting and printing.

UNCIAL

A round version of roman letters dating from the fourth and fifth centuries.

VERSALS

Ornate capitals.

WATERMARK

A translucent mark in paper. A symbol of origin and quality.

WRITING MASTER

After the disintegration of monastic writing schools in the sixteenth century, the tradition was carried on by secular teachers. In central Europe they were active into the eighteenth century.

WRITING SURFACE

Papyrus, parchment, paper.

BIBLIOGRAPHY

BIBLIOGRAPHY

BARTHEL, GUSTAF
Konnte Adam schreiben?
Weltgeschichte der
Schrift
DuMont Schauberg
Köln *1972*

BAUDIN, FERNAND
La Typographie au
Tableaux Noir
Retz
Paris *1984*
How Typography Works
Design Press
New York *1989*

BISCHOFF, BERNHARD
Paläographie des
römischen Altertums
Schmidt
Berlin *1979*

BOCKWITZ, HANS H.
Zur Kulturgeschichte
des Papiers
Feldmühle
Stettin *1935*

BRIEM, GUNNLAUGUR
Italic
The Icelandic Method
Second Hand Press
London *1985*
An illustrated guide. How
the ministry of education
in Reykjavik introduced
the teaching of italic letters
into the curriculum.

BROD, WALTER M.
Fränkische Schreib-
meister und Schreib-
künstler
Mainfränk. Hefte
Würzburg *1968*

BUNZ, WERNER
Quadrata Capitalis
Wittig
Hamburg *1973*

CLAIRBORNE, ROBERT
Die Erfindung der Schrift
Rowohlt
Reinbek bei Hamburg *1978*
Titel der amerik. Ausgabe:
The Birth of Writing
Time Inc.
New York *1974*

COHEN, MARCEL
Die Kunst der Schrift
Unesco Kurier
Paris *1964*

CROUS, ERNST /
KIRCHNER JOACHIM
Die gotischen
Schriftarten
Klinckhardt & Biermann
Leipzig *1928*

DEBES, DIETMAR
Das Figurenalphabet
Dokumentation
München *1968*

DERRIDA, JAQUES
Die Schrift und die
Differenz
Suhrkamp
Frankfurt *1976*
Titel d. franz. Ausgabe:
L'ecriture et la
Difference
Éditions du Seuil *1967*

Writing & Difference
The University of
Chicago Press
Chicago *1978, 1980*

Ders.
Grammatologie
Suhrkamp
Frankfurt am Main *1974*
Titel d. franz. Ausgabe:
De la Grammatologie
Les Éditions de Minuit
Paris *1967*

DOEDE, WERNER
Schön schreiben,
eine Kunst
Joh. Neudörffer und
seine Schule im 16. und
17. Jahrhundert
Prestel
München *1966*

DORTMOND, J.J.
De wereld schreef
Stichting ter Verbetering
van het Handschrift
Lindonk
Amsterdam *1969*

DÜRER, ALBRECHT
Konstruktion der
Antiqua
Majuskeln
Faksimile
Polygraph
Frankfurt am Main *1971*

EHMKE, F.H.
Die historische Entwick-
lung der abendländischen
Schriftformen
Maier
Ravensburg *1927*

Ders.
Schrift
Ihre Gestaltung und
Entwicklung in neuerer
Zeit
Wagner
Hannover *1925*

Ders.
Ziele des
Schriftunterrichts
Ein Beitrag zur modernen
Schriftbewegung
Diederichs
Jena *1911*

EKSCHMITT, WERNER
Das Gedächtnis der Völker
Safari
Berlin / Wien *1968*

FOERSTER, HANS
Abriss der lateinischen
Paläographie
Hiersemann
Stuttgart *1963*

FÖLDES-PAPP. KÁROLYI
Vom Felsbild zum
Alphabet
Belser
Stuttgart *1966*

FICHTENAU, HEINRICH
Die Lehrbücher
Maximilian I. und die
Anfänge der Frakturschrift
Maximilian-Gesellschaft
Hamburg *1961*

FRUTIGER, ADRIAN
HEIDERHOFF, HORST
Der Mensch und seine Zeichen
D. Stempel AG
Frankfurt am Main *1978*

GELB, I.J.
Von der Keilschrift
zum Alphabet.
Grundlagen einer
Schriftwissenschaft
Kohlhammer
Stuttgart *1958*
Titel d. amerik. Ausgabe:
Study of Writing, Rev. ed.
The University of
Chicago Press
Chicago *1963*

GLÜCK, HELMUT
Schrift und Schriftlichkeit
Metzler
Stuttgart *1987*

HARMS, WOLFGANG
Homo viator in bivio
Studien zur Bildlichkeit
des Weges
Fink
München *1970*

HEERMANN, MAGDALENE
*Schreibbewegungstherapie
als Psychotherapieform bei
neurotischen Kindern und
Jugendlichen*
Reinhardt
München / Basel *1977*

HESS, JOSEPH ANTON
*Anweisung zur
Schönschreibkunst*
Faksimile der Handschrift
von 1788
Raecke
Pinneberg *1983*

HOFERICHTER, ERNST
Das wahre Gesicht
Die Handschrift als Spiegel
des Charakters
Kreisselmeyer
München *1966*

HOYER, FRITZ
*Einführung in die
Papierkunde*
Hiersemann
Leipzig *1941*

HUSSEIN, MOHAMED A.
Vom Papyrus zum Codex
Der Beitrag Ägyptens zur
Buchkultur
Edition Leipzig
Leipzig *1970*

IFRAH, GEORGES
*Universalgeschichte der
Zahlen*
Campus
Frankfurt am Main *1986*
Titel d. franz. Ausgabe:
Histoire Universelle des Chiffres
Édition Seghers
Paris *1986*

JACKSON, DONALD
*Die Geschichte vom
Schreiben*
S. Fischer
Frankfurt am Main *1981*
Titel der engl. Ausgabe:
The Story of Writing
Taplinger
New York *1981*

JENSEN, HANS
*Die Schrift
in Vergangenheit und
Gegenwart*
J.J. Augustin
Glückstadt und Hamburg *1937*

JOHNSTON, EDWARD
SIMONS, ANNA (Übers.)
*Schreibschrift,
Zierschrift und
angewandte Schrift*
Klinckhardt & Biermann
Leipzig *1921*

KAPR, ALBERT
NEUDÖRFFER, JOHANN d. Ä.
*Der große Schreibmeister
der deutschen Renaissance*
VEB Harrassowitz
Leipzig *1956*

Ders.
Schriftkunst
Geschichte, Anatomie
und Schönheit der
lateinischen Buchstaben
VEB Verlag der Kunst
Dresden *1965*

KAUTZSCH, RUDOLF
*Wandlungen in der
Schrift und in der Kunst*
Gutenberggesellschaft
Mainz *1929*

Ders.
*Die Entstehung der
Frakturschrift*
Gutenberggesellschaft
Mainz *1922*

KEIM, KARL
Das Papier
Blersch
Stuttgart *1956*

KENYON, FREDERIC SIR
Papyrus
Rohrer
Brünn / Leipzig / Wien
Gedruckt in St. Gallen *1938*
bei H. Tschudy

KLAGES, LUDWIG
Handschrift und Charakter
Joh. Ambrosius Barth
Leipzig *1932*

Ders.
Vom Wesen des Rhythmus
Gropengiesser
Zürich *1944*

Ders.
*Was die Graphologie
nicht kann*
Ein Brief
Speer
Zürich *1949*

KÜHN, HERMANN
LUTZ, MICHEL
Papier
Katalog
Deutsches Museum
München *1986*

KOCH, RUDOLF
Ein Deutscher
Kleine Schriften
Insel
Leipzig *1940*

MERCATOR, Gerardus
Literarum Latinarum
Louvain / Löwen *1540*
Faksimile
Miland
Nieuwkoop 1970

MEYER, HANS Ed.
Die Schriftentwicklung
Graphis Press
Zürich *1959*

MORISON, STANLEY
Schrift / Inschrift / Druck
Hauswedell
Hamburg *1948*

NOORDZIJ, GERRIT
The Stroke of the Pen
Koninglijke Akademie
vor beeldende Kunsten
Den Haag *1983*

Ders.
Das Kind und die Schrift
Typographische Gesellschaft
München *1985*

OSLEY, A.S.
*Scribes and Sources
Handbook of the
Chancery Hand in the
Sixteenth Century*
Texts of Writing Master
Godine
Boston *1980*

254

BIBLIOGRAPHY

RENKER, ARMIN
Das Buch vom Papier
Insel
Leipzig *1934*

SASSOON, ROSEMARY
The Practical Guide to
Children's Handwriting
Thames and Hudson
London *1983*

SENGAI
1750–1837
Katalog
Wien *1964*

SHO
Pinselschrift und Malerei
in Japan 7.–19. Jahrhundert
Katalog
Museen der Stadt Köln *1975*

TECHNISCHE HOCHSCHULE
DARMSTADT
Lehrdruckerei
Atlas zur Geschichte
der Schrift 3 Bde.
Darmstadt *1986*

TROST, VERA
Bibliotheca Palatina
Skriptorium
Heidelberger Bibliotheks-
schriften Nr. 25
Heidelberg *1986*

VAUPEL, ELISABETH
Vom Gänsekiel zur Stahlfeder
Kultur und Technik
Zeitschrift des Deutschen
Museums Heft Nr. 3
München *1986*

WEISS, WISO
Zeittafel zur Papier-
geschichte
VEB Fachbuchverlag *1983*

WESSELY, CARL
Aus der Welt der Papyri
Haessel
Leipzig *1914*

WEULE, KARL
Vom Kerbstock zum Alphabet
Ersatzmittel und Vorstufen
der Schrift
Franckh'sche Verlagshandlung
Stuttgart *1921*

WILLBERG, HANS PETER
NEUFELD, WILHELM
Signaturen
Christians
Hamburg *1977*

Worte in Bewegung
Moderne japanische
Schreibkunst Katalog
Japanisches Kulturinstitut
Köln *1984*

WILLS, FRANZ HERMANN
Schrift und Zeichen
der Völker
von der Urzeit bis
heute
Econ
Düsseldorf/Wien *1977*

ZAPF, HERMANN
WILLIAM, MORRIS
Blanckerts
Scharbeutz *1949*

Ders.
Über Alphabete
Schauer
Frankfurt am Main *1960*

Martin Andersch
Born in Munich in 1921. Studied in Munich
and Hamburg. Worked in cartographic
institutes in Germany, the Netherlands, and
Belgium. Paleographic studies in Germany,
Austria, Switzerland, France, and England.
Three years at sea. Work in publishing since
1950.

Teacher of writing and book art since 1962.
Professor at the University of Hamburg.
Member of Skriptorium Cormoran
Hamburg.

*I do not want art for a few / any more than education
for a few or freedom for a few.*

WILLIAM MORRIS

COLOPHON